PAT BROWN, MBA

SoftballMoney101

Using Softball to Teach the Basics of Money

First published by AbramBrown47 2026

First edition

ISBN: 978-1-967737-52-9

This book was professionally typeset on Reedsy.
Find out more at reedsy.com

Contents

Foreword

Softball has a way of teaching lessons that stick long after the last out is recorded. You learn them early, often without realizing it. Showing up on time. Doing the little things right. Respecting the game. Understanding that talent alone is never enough. You learn that progress comes from repetition, not shortcuts, and that consistency matters more than flashes of brilliance.

Money works the same way.

Many athletes leave the game with discipline, resilience, and work ethic deeply ingrained, yet feel completely unprepared when it comes to managing money. That disconnect is not a failure of the athlete. It is a gap in education. We spend thousands of hours teaching young players how to field a ground ball, read a hitter, or stay composed in a tight game. Very few are ever taught how to read a pay stub, understand a credit score, or make long-term financial decisions with confidence.

This book exists to close that gap.

Softball is a game of preparation and patience. Most games are not won with one swing. They are won by making routine plays, moving runners, executing pitches, and avoiding unforced errors. The best teams trust the process. They understand that one bad inning does not define a season, and one great inning does not guarantee a win. Financial success follows that same rhythm.

You will not find get-rich-quick ideas in these pages. You will find fundamentals. You will find systems. You will find reminders that money, like softball, rewards those who stay disciplined when no one is watching. The habits that made you a reliable teammate and a tough competitor are the same habits that build financial stability over time.

This book speaks to athletes because it respects athletes. It assumes you understand pressure, accountability, and long-term development. It assumes you know what it means to grind through practice, study film, accept coaching, and keep going after setbacks. Those experiences matter. They give you an advantage in money decisions once the rules are explained in a language you already understand.

You may be a current player juggling school, work, and competition. You may be a former player adjusting to life without a structured schedule. You may be someone who never went pro but learned powerful lessons through the game. Wherever you are, the principles in this book apply. Money does not care about trophies or box scores. It responds to preparation, patience, and smart decision-making over time.

Softball also teaches humility. Even the best players fail more than they succeed. That truth carries over into finances. Mistakes will happen. Markets will fluctuate. Life will throw curveballs. What matters is how you respond. Do you panic and abandon the plan, or do you reset, refocus, and trust your training?

This book is not about being perfect with money. It is about being intentional. It is about building a game plan you can stick to through good seasons and bad ones. It is about understanding that financial success is not a single moment, but a series of small, well-executed decisions stacked over time.

If you approach money the way you approached your sport, with respect for fundamentals, openness to coaching, and commitment to daily reps, you will put yourself in a strong position for the long run. You already know how to do hard things. You already know how to compete. This book simply shows you how to apply those strengths to a new arena.

One pitch at a time. One inning at a time. One smart decision after another. That is how games are won. That is how financial confidence is built.

Introduction

No championship season ever unfolds exactly the way it is drawn up on a whiteboard.

There are games where everything clicks and games where nothing does. There are hot streaks, slumps, weather delays, injuries, bad calls, and unexpected heroes. What separates championship teams from everyone else is not perfection. It is the ability to stay locked in when things are messy and keep playing the next pitch the right way.

Softball teaches you early that you cannot control everything. You cannot control the umpire. You cannot control the bounce of the ball. You cannot control the crowd, the weather, or what the other team does. What you can control is your preparation, your effort, and your response. One pitch at a time. One play at a time. One inning at a time.

Money works exactly the same way.

Many athletes approach money the way young players sometimes approach games. They look for a big swing. A quick win. A shortcut that skips the boring fundamentals. When that does not work, frustration sets in. Confidence drops. Bad decisions compound. Just like in softball, pressing rarely leads to good outcomes.

This book is built around a simple idea. Financial success is not about one big moment. It is about stacking small, disciplined decisions over time. Championships are not won with one pitch, and financial independence is not built with one investment.

Athletes are uniquely wired for this approach, even if they do not realize it yet.

You already understand delayed gratification. You trained for years for moments that lasted seconds. You showed up to practice when no one was watching. You trusted coaches, game plans, and systems even when results did not show up immediately. Those same habits apply to money once you understand the rules of the game.

The problem is not effort. Most athletes work harder than the average person. The problem is that no one ever explained money in a way that connects to how athletes actually think and learn. Financial conversations often feel abstract, intimidating, or disconnected from real life. This book changes that by translating financial concepts into the language of the game.

Think about a tight championship game. Bases loaded. No outs. The crowd is loud. The pitcher is locked in. The smartest teams do not panic. They do not swing for the fences unless the situation calls for it. They execute. Move the runner. Make solid contact. Avoid the double play. Trust the process.

Financial decisions live in similar moments.

Do you spend aggressively because everyone else is? Do you abandon your plan because markets are volatile? Do you chase hot investments the way an undisciplined hitter chases bad pitches? Or do you slow the game down, assess the situation, and make the simple play?

This book teaches you how to read those situations.

You will learn how to build a financial game plan that fits your stage of life, income level, and goals. You will learn how to protect yourself from mistakes that cost entire innings. You will learn how to stay disciplined when emotions run high. Most importantly, you will learn how to stay in the game long enough for consistency to work in your favor.

Some readers will have modest incomes. Others may experience sudden opportunities through NIL, bonuses, promotions, or entrepreneurship. The principles do not change. Just like softball fundamentals apply whether you are playing youth ball or college ball, financial fundamentals apply regardless of the size of the paycheck.

This book does not promise easy answers or guaranteed outcomes. Softball never did either. What it offers is a framework. A playbook. A way to think clearly when pressure is high and decisions matter.

There will be chapters where you recognize mistakes you have already made. That is part of the process. Film study is not about shame. It is about learning and adjusting. There will also be chapters that help you get ahead of decisions you have not faced yet. That is preparation, and preparation is how championships are won.

If you commit to approaching money the same way you approached your sport, with humility, discipline, and respect for the fundamentals, you will be far ahead of most people. You do not need to be perfect. You need to stay engaged. You need to keep showing up. You need to play the next pitch the right way.

One pitch at a time is not just a coaching cliché. It is a strategy for winning over the long season of life.

About This Book

Softball is not just a game of talent. It is a game of habits, preparation, and decision-making under pressure. The best players are not always the biggest or strongest. They are the ones who understand situations, trust fundamentals, and stay disciplined when emotions run high. Money rewards those same traits.

This book exists because the lessons softball teaches translate cleanly into how money actually works in the real world.

In softball, you learn quickly that effort alone is not enough. You can work hard all offseason, but if your footwork is sloppy or your swing mechanics are off, the results will show. Money works the same way. You can earn a good income, but without a plan, structure, and discipline, it is easy to stall out or move backward.

Softball also teaches you patience. You do not fix a swing in one cage session. You do not build endurance in one practice. Improvement happens through reps stacked over time. Financial progress follows the same pattern. Saving, investing, and building stability are not one-time decisions. They are habits repeated consistently over seasons.

Another core lesson of softball is situational awareness. A smart player knows the count, the score, the inning, and the runners on base. The same swing does not apply in every situation. Money decisions also depend on context. What makes sense early in your career may not make sense later. What works when income is stable may not work during transitions. This book helps you read the financial scoreboard so you can make smarter plays.

Softball also punishes impatience. Chasing bad pitches leads to weak contact and outs. Financially, chasing hot investments, trends, or quick wins often leads to losses and regret. This book emphasizes consistency over flash, process over outcomes, and discipline over emotion.

One of the most important things softball teaches is accountability. When you miss a cutoff or blow an assignment, it affects the entire team. Money decisions are personal, but their consequences ripple outward. Family, teammates, and future opportunities are impacted by how well you manage what you are given. This book treats money as a responsibility, not a scoreboard for comparison.

Structure matters in softball. Practices are planned. Game plans are reviewed. Film is studied. Money deserves the same respect. This book provides structure without overwhelming you. It breaks financial concepts into manageable pieces, just like drills, so you can build confidence step by step.

You will notice that this book does not rely on fear or hype. It does not assume you want to become an expert investor overnight. It assumes you want clarity, control, and confidence. It assumes you want to avoid unforced errors and put yourself in position to succeed over time.

Softball also teaches resilience. You can do everything right and still lose a game. You can make a great pitch and still give up a hit. That reality applies to money. Markets fluctuate. Life changes. Plans need adjustments. This book teaches you how to stay composed, make smart adjustments, and keep moving forward rather than quitting or panicking.

This is not a book about becoming wealthy at any cost. It is a book about becoming financially steady, confident, and intentional. It is about understanding the rules of the game so money becomes a tool instead of a source of stress.

Whether you played at a high level or simply grew up around the game, softball has already taught you valuable lessons about effort, discipline, and teamwork. This book simply connects those lessons to money in a way that feels familiar and practical.

If you treat your finances the way you treated your training, show up consistently, respect fundamentals, and stay coachable, you will be ahead of most people. Softball prepared you better for this than you might think.

Foolish Assumptions

Every good coach starts with assumptions. Not excuses. Assumptions. They assume you are capable. They assume you can handle responsibility. They assume you are willing to work. This section does the same thing.

These assumptions might feel uncomfortable to some readers. That is intentional. Growth usually starts there.

This book assumes you are competitive. Not just in games, but in life. You care about outcomes. You want to improve. You do not enjoy feeling unprepared or behind. You may not always win, but you hate losing because you were sloppy, undisciplined, or unaware. That mindset matters more than natural talent when it comes to money.

This book assumes you understand effort. You know what it means to show up early, stay late, and repeat drills that are not glamorous. You know that fundamentals win games even when no one is cheering. Money rewards the same behavior. There are no highlight reels for budgeting, saving, or staying invested during boring stretches. This book assumes you are willing to do the uncelebrated work.

This book assumes you can handle honesty. Coaches do not sugarcoat film sessions, and this book will not either. Some financial habits you recognize here may sting a little. That does not mean you failed. It means you are learning. Mistakes are part of development. Refusing to learn from them is the real problem.

This book assumes you are coachable. You may question ideas. You may disagree with certain strategies. That is fine. But this book assumes you are open to learning something new and adjusting when the evidence supports it. The best athletes are not the ones who think they know everything. They are the ones who listen, adapt, and grow.

This book assumes you value consistency over hype. You already know that one great practice does not make a season. One good month of saving does not fix years of bad habits. This book is built on repetition and discipline, not motivation speeches. Motivation fades. Systems last.

This book also assumes you are human. You will make emotional decisions. You will feel pressure to keep up with teammates, friends, or social media. You will sometimes want to force a play instead of trusting the game plan. That does not disqualify you. It just means you need structure and guardrails, the same way teams need rules and accountability.

This book assumes you are responsible for yourself. In sports, playing time is earned. In money, outcomes are earned the same way. Not always fairly. Not always immediately. But over time, patterns show up. This book assumes you are willing to take ownership of your decisions rather than blaming the system, the economy, or bad luck.

This book assumes you care about your future teammates. That might mean a spouse, children, parents, business partners, or friends who rely on you. Financial decisions rarely affect only one person. Just like blown assignments hurt the whole team, financial mistakes ripple outward. This book treats money as stewardship, not ego.

This book assumes you are not looking for shortcuts. If you are hoping for a secret play that guarantees success, this book is not for you. There is no trick pitch that wins every at bat. There is only preparation, discipline, and execution. That truth applies to money as clearly as it does to softball.

Finally, this book assumes you want confidence. Not arrogance. Confidence built on understanding. Confidence that comes from knowing your plan, trusting your process, and staying composed when things get noisy. That kind of confidence is earned, and athletes already know how to earn it.

If these assumptions feel fair, this book will speak your language. If they feel challenging, that is probably a good sign. The work ahead is worth it.

How This Playbook Is Organized

This book is structured the way a good season is structured. There is a plan, a progression, and a purpose behind the order of everything. You do not start the season with trick plays or advanced schemes. You start with fundamentals. You build confidence. You layer complexity as skills improve. That same logic guides how this playbook is organized.

Each part of this book represents a phase of development, much like a training cycle, a season, and a career.

The early sections focus on awareness and basics. Before you can execute a game plan, you need to understand the scoreboard. Where are you right now. What resources do you have. What mistakes are costing you outs. These chapters are about clarity, not judgment. You cannot fix what you refuse to measure, and you cannot improve what you do not understand.

As the book progresses, the focus shifts from defense to offense. Just like in softball, protecting yourself from mistakes comes before taking calculated risks. Learning how to manage cash flow, credit, insurance, and basic protection keeps you in the game when things go wrong. This is the equivalent of solid defense and smart pitching. It may not be flashy, but it wins games.

Once that foundation is in place, the book moves into investing fundamentals. This section emphasizes consistency over heroics. You will learn how markets work, how risk and return relate to one another, and why long-term discipline beats short-term excitement. The softball analogy stays front and center. Making consistent contact, trusting your mechanics, and sticking to the plan matter far more than chasing highlight-reel moments.

Later chapters focus on managing the game over time. Just like a good coach makes adjustments without panicking, these sections teach you how to review, rebalance, and refine your financial plan as life changes. Careers evolve. Income fluctuates. Priorities shift. The goal is not to constantly overhaul your plan, but to make smart, intentional adjustments when they are needed.

The final sections zoom out to the full season and beyond. Money decisions do not exist in isolation. Taxes, housing, careers, family, and legacy all intersect. These chapters help you think beyond the next game and prepare for long-term success. This is where the playbook connects money to life, not just accounts and numbers.

Every chapter follows a consistent structure so you know what to expect, just like a well-run practice. Chapters open with a softball-based story or scenario that sets the tone and stakes. From there, financial concepts are explained through the lens of the game, using clear comparisons that feel natural to athletes.

You will also see sections framed from a coach's perspective. These are intentional. Coaches reinforce habits through repetition, simple language, and accountability. Money benefits from the same approach. Expect reminders about discipline, patience, effort, and avoiding emotional mistakes. If it feels like something a coach would say in practice or a locker room, that is by design.

Many chapters include realistic game situations that mirror real financial decisions. These moments are meant to slow things down and make you think. Do you force a play, or do you trust the system. Do you react emotionally, or do you stay composed. Each scenario is tied directly back to a money lesson you can apply immediately.

At the end of every chapter, you will find an Athlete Takeaways section. These are not summaries. They are reminders. Short, direct lessons written in sports language that you can carry with you. Think of them like cues written on a wristband or phrases a coach repeats all season. Simple. Clear. Actionable.

You do not need to read this book in one sitting. Just like training, progress happens through steady reps. You can move chapter by chapter, reflect, and apply what you learn as you go. The goal is not to rush to the end. The goal is to build confidence and consistency over time.

This playbook is not about winning one game. It is about building habits that hold up over an entire season and beyond.

About Pat Brown

Pat Brown's approach to money, discipline, and long-term success was shaped long before he entered the financial world. It was built in locker rooms, weight rooms, meeting rooms, and seasons where preparation mattered more than promises.

Pat played college football at the University of Kansas from 1994 to 1999 and was named team captain for the 1999 season. Those years instilled values that translate cleanly across all sports, including softball. Accountability. Preparation. Doing your job. Showing up every day whether you feel like it or not. Competing with discipline instead of ego. Those lessons remain the foundation of his work today.

After his playing career ended, Pat transitioned into financial services and built a career as a financial advisor and wealth manager. He works with individuals, families, business owners, and athletes who are navigating increasingly complex financial lives. His work focuses on helping people make smart decisions around cash flow, investing, retirement planning, tax strategy, and philanthropy, especially during periods of transition.

Pat pursued advanced education alongside his professional experience, earning an MBA and multiple industry designations, including ChFC®, RICP®, and CAP®. His background blends formal training with real-world application, recognizing that money decisions rarely happen in calm, controlled environments. They happen under pressure, uncertainty, and emotion, conditions athletes understand well.

As the college sports landscape changed with the introduction of Name, Image, and Likeness opportunities, Pat saw a familiar problem emerging. Student athletes were gaining access to income, contracts, and endorsements without the financial fundamentals needed to manage taxes, budgeting, business structures, and long-term consequences. Many were being asked to make adult financial decisions without ever being taught the rules.

That gap became the catalyst for Pat's work in athlete financial education.

Rather than approaching athletes with spreadsheets and jargon, Pat focused on translating financial concepts into language athletes already understand. Preparation. Reps. Game plans. Adjustments. Discipline over time. His goal has always been simple. Help athletes avoid unforced errors and stay in the game long enough for consistency to work in their favor.

Pat has since become a recognized voice in athlete financial education and has been featured by national publications and platforms including Financial Planning, Yahoo, and ESPN Andscape. His work centers on financial literacy gaps, NIL planning, and the real challenges facing student athletes and their families as opportunity arrives faster than education.

These experiences led Pat to author a series of practical, athlete-focused books designed to meet athletes and families where they are. His NIL-related titles include Financial Literacy for NIL, Financial Literacy for NIL for Parents of Student Athletes, Financial Literacy for NIL for High School Students, and Financial Literacy for NIL for International Student Athletes. Each book emphasizes clarity, realism, and fundamentals rather than theory or hype.

Pat also created a growing collection of sport-specific financial education books, including Football Money 101, Baseball Money 101, Basketball Money 101, Cheer Money 101, Dance Money 101, Gymnastics Money 101, Hockey Money 101, Lacrosse Money 101, Rowing Money 101, Soccer Money 101, Softball Money 101, Tennis Money 101, Track Money 101, Volleyball Money 101, and Wrestling Money 101. Each title is written to reflect the culture, rhythm, and demands of the sport while teaching financial lessons athletes can apply long after competition ends.

Softball Money 101 is built on the same philosophy. Softball rewards repetition, patience, situational awareness, and mental toughness. Games are rarely decided by one swing. They are won by execution, fundamentals, and avoiding mistakes that cost innings. Money works the same way, and this book connects those dots clearly and intentionally.

To extend this mission beyond books, Pat founded Former Student Athlete, a platform created to support athletes navigating life after sports. The platform focuses on financial literacy, career transitions, health, identity, and long-term success once the uniform comes off. You can learn more at www.formerstudentathlete.com, www.financialliteracyfornil.com, and www.financialliteracyforstudentathletes.com.

Pat's work is rooted in a belief shaped by both sports and finance. Athletes deserve a better playbook for life after competition, and financial education should arrive before opportunity turns into regret.

Part I: Fundamentals and First Pitch

You cannot win games without mastering the basics.

Every season starts the same way. Before tournaments, before rivalry games, before championships, teams return to fundamentals. Grip. Footwork. Throws. Timing. Communication. No matter how experienced the roster is, the basics get revisited because coaches know something athletes sometimes forget. When pressure rises, you fall back on fundamentals, not flashy skills.

Money works the same way.

Most financial mistakes are not caused by complex strategies or advanced investing concepts. They come from skipping the basics. Not knowing where money is going. Not understanding how credit works. Not having cash set aside for emergencies. Not having a system. When those fundamentals are missing, even good income and good intentions cannot save you.

This first section of the book is about building your foundation.

In softball, the first pitch of the game sets the tone. It does not decide the outcome, but it tells you a lot. Is the pitcher composed. Is the defense ready. Is the team locked in or sloppy. Financially, your first pitch is awareness. Understanding where you stand right now. Income. Expenses. Debt. Savings. Accounts. Nothing improves until you are honest about the starting point.

Many athletes avoid this step because it feels uncomfortable. Looking at numbers can feel like watching film of a bad game. But just like film, clarity is power. You cannot adjust what you refuse to look at.

This section focuses on fundamentals that keep you in the game when things get hard. Cash flow. Budgeting. Banking. Credit. Debt. These are not exciting topics, but neither are defensive drills. They are essential. Teams that skip them get exposed quickly. So do people.

You will learn how to create simple systems that work in real life, not perfect spreadsheets that fall apart under pressure. You will learn how to automate good behavior the same way practice schedules force consistency. You will learn why emergency funds matter the same way injury prevention matters. Not because you expect something to go wrong, but because eventually something will.

This section also addresses a reality many athletes face after their playing days end. The structure disappears. Practices are gone. Coaches stop checking in. The calendar opens up. Without structure, even disciplined people drift. Money needs structure to replace what sports once provided. Systems become your new coach.

Another key focus of this section is avoiding unforced errors. In softball, errors extend innings, increase pitch counts, and shift momentum. Financially, overdraft fees, high-interest debt, missed payments, and poor banking decisions do the same thing. You do not need to out-earn every problem. You need to stop creating avoidable ones.

Fundamentals also build confidence. When you trust your mechanics, you play freer. When you understand your finances, decisions feel less emotional. You stop reacting and start executing. That is what this section aims to give you.

This part of the book does not ask you to be perfect. It asks you to be consistent. Show up. Do the reps. Build habits that hold up over time. Just like in softball, fundamentals do not guarantee wins, but without them, losses are almost guaranteed.

By the end of this section, you should feel grounded. Not overwhelmed. You should understand the basic rules of the money game and how to operate within them. From there, everything else builds more smoothly.

You cannot hit home runs without a stance. You cannot win championships without fundamentals. The same is true with money. This is where the work starts.

Chapter 1: Why Money Feels Confusing After Softball

Every softball player remembers a moment like this.

You have trained for years. Practices, lifts, conditioning, film, travel ball, tournaments, long weekends, early mornings. Your schedule was full, your role was clear, and expectations were constant. Then one season ends, or your playing career ends altogether, and suddenly the structure disappears.

No practice schedule. No coach checking in. No game plan posted on the locker room wall.

Just real life.

Money often enters the picture at the same time. A paycheck. A stipend. NIL income. A signing bonus. A new job. And instead of feeling confident, many athletes feel lost. Not because they lack discipline, but because they were never taught how this game works.

That confusion is not your fault. It is a predictable outcome of how athletes are developed.

Why Financial Literacy Is Rarely Taught to Athletes

Athletes spend most of their formative years being trained for performance, not preparation for life after the sport. Coaches focus on what wins games now. Parents focus on schedules, logistics, and opportunities. Schools focus on eligibility and academics tied to competition.

Money rarely makes the list.

The system assumes someone else will teach it later. Parents assume schools will handle it. Schools assume families will handle it. Teams assume athletes will figure it out when they need to. By the time money becomes real, the education gap is already there.

Softball players are trained to follow structure. You knew where to be, when to be there, and what was expected. Money does not come with that same structure by default. No one hands you a playbook explaining taxes, budgeting, credit, or investing. You are expected to learn by trial and error.

That would be like throwing a freshman into a championship game without ever teaching them the rules.

Money Myths Passed Through Dugouts and Travel Teams

When formal education is missing, myths fill the gap.

In softball circles, money advice often comes from teammates, parents, social media, or stories about someone who made it big. These myths spread the same way bad mechanics do. They sound confident. They get repeated. And they lead to mistakes.

Some common ones sound like this.

"If you make good money, you do not need a plan."

"That investment worked for my friend, so it should work for me."

"Saving is for people who do not make much."

"Real money is made by taking big risks."

These are the financial equivalent of swinging at every pitch because you hit one home run once. It ignores context, timing, and consistency.

Athletes understand that advice without context is dangerous on the field. The same is true with money. What works for one person in one situation may be completely wrong for someone else.

Saving vs Investing vs Gambling

One reason money feels confusing is because different behaviors get lumped together as if they are the same thing.

They are not.

Saving is defense. It is about protection and stability. Emergency funds, short-term goals, and cash reserves exist to keep you in the game when something goes wrong. In softball terms, this is solid defense and smart pitching. It does not get headlines, but it prevents disasters.

Investing is offense with a plan. It is about long-term growth, patience, and trusting systems over time. It is not about winning every day. It is about positioning yourself to succeed over seasons. This is like consistent contact, moving runners, and letting the lineup do its job.

Gambling is swinging without a plan. It is chasing outcomes without understanding risk, probabilities, or consequences. It feels exciting, especially when it works once. But over time, it costs innings, games, and seasons.

Many athletes confuse investing with gambling because both involve uncertainty. The difference is discipline. Investing respects time, diversification, and process. Gambling ignores them.

Softball players already understand this distinction. A disciplined hitter has an approach. A gambler swings at whatever looks exciting. Over time, one lasts. The other does not.

Why Consistency Beats Swinging for the Fences

Softball rewards consistency more than raw power. The best teams are not always the ones with the most home runs. They are the ones that limit mistakes, put pressure on opponents, and execute repeatedly.

Money works the same way.

Most financial success does not come from one big decision. It comes from many small ones done correctly over time. Paying yourself first. Investing consistently. Avoiding high-interest debt. Staying patient during volatility. None of these are exciting, but they work.

Athletes often struggle here because they are wired for competition and immediate feedback. Money does not always give that. Progress can feel slow. Results are not always visible. That leads some people to abandon the plan and chase something louder.

That is the financial version of pressing at the plate.

Consistency requires trust. Trust in the process. Trust in systems. Trust that boring done well beats exciting done poorly. Softball teaches this lesson every season. Players who show up daily, do their reps, and stay disciplined usually outperform those who rely on talent alone.

Coach's Perspective: What Would Your Coach Say?

A good coach would not complicate this.

They would say things like:

"Do your job."

"Reps matter."

"Don't cheat the work."

"Trust the process."

"Make the simple play."

Financially, that translates to knowing where your money goes, building basic systems, and sticking to them even when emotions kick in. It means not forcing plays when things feel slow. It means not abandoning fundamentals because someone else hit a highlight-reel home run.

Coaches care about effort, but they also care about execution. Money requires both.

Game Situations and Decision Points

Situation one. You receive unexpected income. Do you spend it immediately because it feels earned, or do you pause, assess your needs, and make a plan?

Situation two. Markets drop and everyone is talking about it. Do you panic and pull out, or do you stay composed and trust your long-term strategy?

Situation three. A friend is making fast money doing something risky. Do you chase it, or do you stick to what fits your plan?

Each situation mirrors a softball moment. Do you force a swing, or do you stay within yourself?

Common Athlete Mistakes and Financial Parallels

Athletes often press when results are slow. Financially, that shows up as chasing quick wins.

Athletes sometimes ignore fundamentals because they feel beneath them. Financially, that shows up as skipping budgeting or saving.

Athletes sometimes compare themselves to teammates. Financially, that shows up as lifestyle inflation and unnecessary spending.

The parallels are clear, and they are correctable.

Winning the Long Game

Money feels confusing after softball because the structure disappeared, not because you lack discipline or intelligence. This book rebuilds that structure using a language you already understand.

You already know how to train. You already know how to trust a process. You already know how to bounce back after mistakes.

This chapter is the reset. The reminder that fundamentals still matter. That consistency still wins. That you do not need to swing for the fences to build something meaningful.

You just need to play the next pitch the right way.

Athlete Takeaways

- Fundamentals win seasons, not highlight plays
- Saving is defense, investing is offense, gambling is chaos
- Consistency beats pressing, every time
- Systems replace structure when the season ends
- Play money one pitch at a time

Chapter 2: Read the Scoreboard: Your Financial Snapshot

Every softball player knows the importance of the scoreboard, even if they do not stare at it constantly.

You glance up between pitches. Inning. Outs. Score. Count. Who is on base. The scoreboard does not tell you how to feel, but it tells you the truth. You cannot play the game well if you are guessing about the situation.

Now imagine trying to play without it.

You do not know if you are winning or losing. You are unsure how many outs there are. You do not know if you need to be aggressive or patient. That confusion leads to forced plays and mental mistakes.

That is exactly how most people operate with money.

They work hard, earn income, and make decisions without ever reading the scoreboard. They are busy, not informed. They feel stressed, not clear. This chapter is about changing that.

Income, Expenses, and Cash Flow

In softball, runs matter, but how they are created matters too. A team that scores once but gives up three is not winning. Money works the same way.

Income is what comes in. Paychecks, stipends, NIL deals, bonuses, side work. Expenses are what go out. Rent, food, gas, subscriptions, travel, insurance. Cash flow is the difference between the two.

Positive cash flow means more is coming in than going out. Negative cash flow means the opposite.

Many athletes focus only on income. They assume that if they make enough money, things will work themselves out. That is rarely true. Plenty of people with strong income struggle because they never controlled expenses.

Cash flow is not about judgment. It is about awareness. Just like knowing whether you are ahead or behind in a game changes strategy, knowing your cash flow changes decisions.

If you do not know this number, you are playing blind.

Assets, Liabilities, and Net Worth

Softball teams know their roster. Who can hit. Who can pitch. Who plays defense. You cannot build a lineup without knowing what you have.

Financially, assets are what you own. Cash, savings, investments, retirement accounts, property. Liabilities are what you owe. Credit cards, student loans, car loans, personal loans.

Net worth is assets minus liabilities.

This is not a score of your value as a person. It is a snapshot of your position. Early in life, many athletes have a low or negative net worth. That is normal. What matters is direction and improvement over time.

Tracking this is like tracking team stats. It shows progress, trends, and areas that need work.

Fixed vs Variable Expenses

Not all expenses behave the same way, and understanding this is like understanding the difference between controllable and uncontrollable plays.

Fixed expenses are predictable. Rent. Insurance premiums. Loan payments. These do not change much month to month.

Variable expenses move. Food. Travel. Entertainment. Clothing. Subscriptions. These are where most people lose control without realizing it.

Athletes understand this concept intuitively. Some things are built into the schedule. Others depend on choices. If you treat every expense like it is fixed, you lose flexibility. If you ignore fixed expenses, you create stress.

This chapter helps you separate the two so adjustments become possible.

Reviewing Where Your Money Actually Goes

This is the film session.

Most people think they know where their money goes. Most are wrong.

Small expenses stack. Subscriptions go unnoticed. Convenience spending adds up. None of this is evil. It is just invisible without review.

Reviewing spending is not about cutting joy. It is about intentionality. In softball, watching film is not punishment. It is how improvement happens. You spot tendencies. You clean up mistakes. You make better decisions next time.

Money deserves the same respect.

Look back at the last three months. Not one week. Patterns matter more than one-off events. Where is money leaking? Where is it aligned with your priorities? Where is it just habit?

This step alone creates clarity and often relief.

The Investing Concept Explained Through the Sport

In softball, strategy depends on the situation. Early innings are different from late innings. A one-run game is different from a blowout.

Financially, your snapshot informs strategy.

If cash flow is tight, defense matters more than offense. If you have positive cash flow and stability, offense becomes possible. If debt is high, cleanup matters. If savings are strong, flexibility increases.

You cannot skip this step and jump into investing without understanding risk. That would be like calling aggressive plays without knowing the score.

Coach's Perspective: What Would Your Coach Say?

A coach would keep this simple.

"Know the situation."

"Pay attention."

"Details matter."

"The scoreboard doesn't lie."

Financially, this means knowing your numbers, not guessing. It means checking in regularly, not once a year. It means taking responsibility for awareness, even when it is uncomfortable.

Coaches expect effort, but they also expect awareness. You cannot fix what you refuse to look at.

Game Situations and Decision Points

Situation one. You get a raise. Do you immediately upgrade your lifestyle, or do you check how it changes your cash flow?

Situation two. You feel stressed about money but do not know why. Do you ignore it, or do you review your spending patterns?

Situation three. You want to invest but have no idea how much you can afford. Do you guess, or do you read the scoreboard first?

Each situation mirrors a softball moment. Awareness comes before action.

Common Athlete Mistakes and Financial Parallels

Athletes often rely on feel instead of data. Financially, that shows up as guessing instead of tracking.

Athletes sometimes avoid film when results are bad. Financially, that shows up as ignoring statements and balances.

Athletes sometimes confuse activity with progress. Financially, that shows up as working harder without better systems.

These are correctable once awareness exists.

Winning the Long Game

Reading the scoreboard does not win games by itself. But teams that ignore it almost always lose.

This chapter is about clarity, not control. Once you understand where you are, decisions get easier. Stress decreases. Confidence builds.

You do not need perfect numbers. You need honest ones.

This snapshot is not permanent. It will change. That is the point. But you cannot manage the game if you do not know the situation.

Read the scoreboard. Then play the next pitch accordingly.

Athlete Takeaways

- Know the score before you change the strategy
- Cash flow tells you more than income ever will
- Assets and liabilities are just a roster, not a judgment
- Film study creates improvement, not shame
- Awareness comes before execution

Chapter 3: Playing Small Ball: Budgeting and Saving

Championship teams rarely rely on one swing to win a game.

They bunt runners over. They hit behind the runner. They take the extra base when it is there. They force the defense to make plays. Small ball is not flashy, but it applies pressure every inning. Over time, it wears teams down and puts wins on the board.

Money works the same way.

Most people think financial success comes from a big moment. A big raise. A big investment. A big break. In reality, it is built through small, disciplined actions repeated consistently. Budgeting and saving are the financial version of small ball. They do not look exciting, but they win seasons.

Budgeting Systems That Actually Work

Budgeting has a bad reputation, especially among athletes. It sounds restrictive. It feels like someone telling you what you cannot do. That is not what good budgeting is.

In softball terms, a budget is a game plan. It tells you where to be, what your role is, and how to allocate resources. A bad game plan feels suffocating. A good one creates freedom because everyone knows what to expect.

Budgeting only works if it is simple enough to stick with under pressure. Complicated spreadsheets are like trick plays that fall apart when the game speeds up.

The best systems share a few traits.

They are realistic. They reflect how you actually live, not how you wish you lived.

They are flexible. One bad week does not break the plan.

They are repeatable. You can follow them even when life gets busy.

Some athletes like the pay-yourself-first approach. Money is automatically set aside for saving and investing, and the rest is what you live on. Others prefer category-based systems where spending is tracked loosely rather than obsessively. The specific system matters less than consistency.

Budgeting is not about perfection. It is about awareness and intention. Just like practice plans adjust throughout the season, your budget can evolve as your life changes.

Automating Savings Like Daily Reps

Athletes understand reps. You do not think your way into better performance. You train your way there.

Saving works the same way.

If saving depends on willpower, it will fail under stress. Travel, social pressure, busy schedules, and fatigue all compete for attention. Automation removes decision-making from the equation.

Automatic transfers to savings or investment accounts are the financial equivalent of scheduled practice. You do not debate whether to show up. You just do.

Even small amounts matter. Ten or twenty dollars saved consistently beats big deposits made once in a while. Over time, those reps stack. Confidence grows. Habits form.

Automation also reduces regret. Money that never hits your checking account is money you never feel tempted to spend. That is not deprivation. That is discipline.

Emergency Funds as Injury Protection

Every athlete understands injury risk.

You do not plan to get hurt. You train to avoid it. You stretch. You lift. You recover. But you still respect the possibility.

An emergency fund is financial injury protection.

It exists to cover unexpected expenses like medical bills, car repairs, job changes, or delayed income. Without it, small problems become major setbacks. With it, you stay in the game.

Many athletes resist building emergency funds because it feels unproductive. Cash does not grow fast. It just sits there.

That is missing the point.

Emergency funds are not about growth. They are about survival and flexibility. They prevent you from taking on bad debt or selling investments at the wrong time. They protect momentum.

Think of it like depth on the roster. You hope you do not need it, but when something goes wrong, you are grateful it is there.

Balancing Lifestyle With Long-Term Goals

Athletes often struggle with balance when money starts coming in.

There is pressure to reward yourself. To keep up with teammates. To enjoy the moment. None of that is wrong. The problem is when short-term enjoyment crowds out long-term progress.

In softball, players know the difference between playing loose and playing careless. Confidence does not mean ignoring fundamentals. It means trusting them.

Financially, balance means spending intentionally. Enjoying life while still building toward future goals. You do not need to live like a monk to be responsible. You need boundaries.

Ask simple questions.

Does this spending align with what I value?

Would I still feel good about this choice six months from now?

Is this a reward, or is it avoidance?

Small ball is about discipline. It is about making the smart play even when something flashier is available.

The Investing Concept Explained Through the Sport

Small ball in softball keeps innings alive. It creates opportunities without forcing outcomes.

Budgeting and saving do the same thing financially.

They create optionality. They give you choices. They allow you to take advantage of opportunities when they appear instead of reacting out of panic.

People who skip these steps often feel trapped. Every decision feels urgent. Every setback feels catastrophic. Small ball prevents that.

Coach's Perspective: What Would Your Coach Say?

A coach would not overcomplicate this.

"Do your job."

"Reps matter."

"Details win games."

"Don't beat yourself."

Financially, this means showing up consistently. Making saving automatic. Avoiding unforced errors. Trusting boring fundamentals.

Coaches know championships are built on habits, not speeches. Money works the same way.

Game Situations and Decision Points

Situation one. You get paid and feel tempted to spend first and save later. Do you flip the order or stick to automation?

Situation two. An unexpected expense hits. Do you panic and use credit, or do you tap your emergency fund and stay composed?

Situation three. Friends are spending aggressively. Do you follow, or do you stay aligned with your goals?

Each situation mirrors a softball decision. Do you force a play, or do you take the smart out?

Common Athlete Mistakes and Financial Parallels

Athletes sometimes ignore small details because they want big results. Financially, that shows up as skipping budgeting.

Athletes sometimes rely on motivation instead of systems. Financially, that shows up as inconsistent saving.

Athletes sometimes reward themselves too early. Financially, that shows up as lifestyle inflation.

These mistakes are common, and they are fixable.

Winning the Long Game

Small ball does not win headlines, but it wins championships.

Budgeting and saving build confidence. They reduce stress. They create momentum. Over time, they make investing easier and decisions clearer.

You do not need to be perfect. You need to be consistent.

Make the simple play. Take the extra base. Trust the process.

That is how you stay in the game long enough to win.

Athlete Takeaways

- Small ball wins seasons, not one swing
- Automation beats motivation every time
- Emergency funds keep you in the game
- Balance spending with purpose, not pressure
- Stack good reps and trust the process

Chapter 4: Credit, Debt, and Avoiding Errors

Ask any coach what drives them crazy, and errors will be near the top of the list.

Not because mistakes never happen. They do. But because many errors are preventable. A rushed throw. Poor footwork. Not calling the ball. Those mistakes extend innings, raise pitch counts, and hand momentum to the other team. Talent does not fix them. Fundamentals do.

Credit and debt work the same way.

Most financial stress is not caused by lack of income. It is caused by unforced errors around credit. Missed payments. High interest. Poor understanding of how the system works. These mistakes quietly cost innings and sometimes entire games. They add pressure, limit options, and force people into reactive decisions.

This chapter is about learning the rules so you stop beating yourself.

How Credit Scores and Reports Work

A credit score is not a judgment of character. It is a performance metric.

Think of it like a stat line. It reflects how you have handled credit over time. On-time payments, balances, length of history, and types of credit all factor in. No single play defines it. Patterns do.

Paying on time consistently matters more than almost anything else. Carrying high balances hurts. Opening and closing accounts too frequently adds noise. Length of history rewards patience. These are not opinions. They are rules.

Your credit report is the film.

It shows your accounts, payment history, balances, and inquiries. Errors happen. Accounts get reported incorrectly. Old mistakes linger longer than they should. If you never review the film, you never see the blown assignments.

Softball players watch film to clean up mechanics. Reviewing your credit report does the same thing. It shows where things went wrong, what needs attention, and what is actually helping you.

Consistency wins here. One great month does not erase years of missed payments. One mistake does not ruin everything if it is followed by disciplined play. Credit rewards habits, not heroics.

Credit Cards, Loans, and Interest

Credit cards and loans are tools.

Used correctly, they create flexibility. Used poorly, they create pressure.

Interest is the cost of borrowing. When you carry balances, interest works against you every day. It compounds quietly. It is like starting every inning with runners already on base. You can still get out of it, but everything is harder.

Credit cards are not free money. They are short-term loans with high penalties for mistakes. Used responsibly, they build credit, provide convenience, and offer protections. Used carelessly, they drain momentum and trap cash flow.

Loans follow the same pattern.

Some loans support long-term progress. Education that increases earning potential. A reasonable mortgage. A reliable vehicle needed for work. These can make sense if they fit your income and plan.

Other loans fund impulse spending. Lifestyle upgrades. Short-term satisfaction with long-term cost. These usually create drag that lasts far longer than the enjoyment.

Understanding interest changes behavior. It turns vague stress into clear math. Just like knowing the count changes how you approach a pitch, knowing the true cost of borrowing changes decisions.

Good Debt vs Bad Debt

Not all debt is equal.

Good debt supports growth or stability. It has a clear purpose and a realistic payoff plan. Even then, good debt still needs management. A mortgage that fits your income is different from one that stretches you thin. Education debt that leads to higher earnings is different from debt taken without a plan.

Bad debt usually funds consumption without lasting value.

High-interest credit cards. Financing clothes, trips, or gadgets. Lifestyle upgrades that feel good briefly and hurt for years. This kind of debt creates pressure without progress.

Athletes understand this instinctively.

Some risks are calculated. You take them because the upside fits the situation. Others are reckless. They ignore context and consequences. Knowing the difference keeps you in the game.

Debt itself is not the enemy. Unmanaged debt is.

Debt Mistakes That Cost Innings

Most debt problems do not start with one big mistake. They start with small ones repeated.

Missing payments is the fastest way to damage credit. Even one missed payment can lower your score and trigger fees and higher interest rates.

Carrying high balances increases interest costs and hurts credit utilization. It signals stress, even if income is strong.

Opening accounts without a plan creates confusion. Too many cards or loans increase the chance of missed payments and poor tracking.

Ignoring statements allows small problems to grow. Fraud, errors, and creeping balances go unnoticed until damage is done.

These are financial errors. They rarely cause immediate disaster. But they extend innings. They raise pitch counts. They shift momentum away from you.

Just like in softball, one error rarely ends a game. A pattern of them does.

The Investing Concept Explained Through the Sport

Credit and debt affect everything that comes later.

High-interest debt limits flexibility. It makes saving harder. It delays investing. It forces short-term thinking. Solid credit creates options. It lowers borrowing costs. It expands opportunity.

Think of credit as field position.

Good field position gives you choices. You can call different plays. You can take smart risks. Bad field position forces you to play defense constantly. You are reacting instead of controlling the game.

Investing works best when credit and debt are under control. Not perfect. Controlled.

Coach's Perspective: What Would Your Coach Say?

A coach would be blunt.

"Don't beat yourself."

"Make the routine play."

"Know the rules."

"Details matter."

Financially, this means paying on time, understanding interest, and not using credit emotionally. Coaches hate preventable mistakes. Credit mistakes fall into that category.

Discipline here prevents bigger problems later.

Game Situations and Decision Points

Situation one. You want something now, but you do not have the cash. Do you use credit without a plan or wait until it fits?

Situation two. You are carrying a balance and feel stuck. Do you ignore it and hope it goes away, or do you build a payoff strategy and regain control?

Situation three. You see a great offer for a new card. Do you open it impulsively or evaluate how it fits your system and goals?

Each decision mirrors a softball moment. Do you rush the throw or set your feet? Do you force a play or take the sure out?

Common Athlete Mistakes and Financial Parallels

Athletes sometimes rush plays under pressure. Financially, that shows up as impulse credit use.

Athletes sometimes ignore fundamentals when tired. Financially, that shows up as missed payments and sloppy tracking.

Athletes sometimes try to make up for mistakes with risk. Financially, that shows up as taking on more debt to fix old debt.

Awareness fixes these patterns. Systems reinforce it.

Automatic payments. Clear limits. Fewer accounts. Regular reviews. These are financial fundamentals.

Winning the Long Game

Credit and debt do not win games. They prevent losses.

When managed well, they stay quiet. When mismanaged, they dominate everything. They affect stress, sleep, and decision-making far beyond the numbers.

This chapter is about control.

Knowing the rules. Avoiding unforced errors. Protecting momentum so you can focus on progress instead of cleanup.

Make the routine plays. Stay disciplined. Let the game come to you.

Athlete Takeaways

- Credit is a stat line, not a character judgment
- Interest punishes mistakes every day
- Good debt supports progress, bad debt creates drag
- Missed payments cost innings fast
- Discipline beats damage control

Chapter 5: The Equipment Bag of Money: Banking Basics

Every softball player knows what happens when the equipment bag is a mess.

You are digging around looking for your glove while warmups are starting. Your cleats are still wet from the last game. One batting glove is missing. Nothing feels smooth, and frustration sets in before the first pitch is even thrown. You feel rushed, off-balance, and distracted. Not because you forgot how to play, but because the basics are not in order.

The problem is not talent. It is organization.

Banking works the same way.

When your money is scattered, poorly organized, or misunderstood, everything feels harder than it needs to be. Bills get missed. Transfers get delayed. You hesitate before spending because you are not sure what is safe. Stress increases, and small mistakes compound. This chapter is about organizing your money the same way you organize your gear so it works for you, not against you.

Good banking does not make you rich. But bad banking makes everything else harder.

Checking vs Savings Accounts

Checking accounts are for movement. Savings accounts are for storage.

A checking account is where income lands and bills get paid. It is the account you swipe, tap, and use daily. Think of it as your everyday glove. It should be reliable, familiar, and easy to access. You do not want surprises here. You want clarity.

Savings accounts serve a different purpose. They are for protection and short-term goals. Emergency funds. Planned expenses. Buffer money. This is backup gear. You may not use it every inning, but when you need it, you really need it.

Problems arise when these roles get mixed.

When savings sit in checking, they tend to get spent. It feels available, so it gets treated like spending money. When checking money sits in savings, access becomes awkward, and people end up moving money back and forth constantly.

Separation creates clarity.

Good systems give each dollar a job. Checking handles flow. Savings handles protection. When you respect those roles, decisions get easier and mistakes decrease.

Online Banks vs Traditional Banks

Not all banks operate the same way, and choosing one is like choosing equipment.

Traditional banks offer branches, in-person service, and familiarity. You can walk in, talk to someone, and handle things face to face. For some people, that comfort matters, especially for complex situations.

Online banks operate differently. They often offer higher interest on savings accounts, lower fees, and better digital tools. The tradeoff is that there are no physical branches.

Neither option is universally better.

The right choice depends on how you use your money. Some people value in-person access. Others value efficiency, automation, and higher savings rates.

Many athletes use a hybrid approach. Checking at a traditional bank for convenience and accessibility. Savings at an online bank for better returns and separation. The goal is function, not loyalty.

Banks are tools. Choose the ones that support your habits instead of fighting them.

How Money Moves Electronically

Understanding how money moves prevents confusion and errors.

Direct deposit sends income straight into your account. Transfers move money between your own accounts. Electronic payments handle bills, subscriptions, and everyday expenses.

What matters is timing.

Money does not always move instantly. Some transfers clear the same day. Others take one to three business days. Weekends and holidays slow things down. Pending transactions can make balances look higher than they actually are.

This is where many overdrafts happen.

Athletes understand timing intuitively. You need to know when the ball arrives and when the runner is actually safe. Guessing leads to errors.

Knowing when money truly clears, not just when it appears on a screen, helps you avoid mistakes. It allows you to plan payments, transfers, and spending with confidence instead of hope.

Protecting Yourself From Fraud and Overdrafts

Fraud and overdrafts are common, and both are largely preventable.

Fraud happens when information is exposed, reused, or poorly monitored. Strong passwords, two-factor authentication, and alerts dramatically reduce risk. Reviewing accounts regularly helps you catch issues early, before damage spreads.

Ignoring accounts is like never checking your gear. Small problems turn into big ones.

Overdrafts happen when spending exceeds available funds. Fees stack quickly, and repeated overdrafts create unnecessary stress. Alerts, buffers, and awareness prevent most of these issues.

Banks offer tools for a reason. Balance alerts. Transaction alerts. Low-balance warnings. These are not annoyances. They are safeguards.

Think of alerts like a coach calling out reminders from the dugout. They keep you aware before mistakes happen.

The Investing Concept Explained Through the Sport

Banking is infrastructure.

It does not win games. It does not create highlights. But without it, nothing else works. You cannot save consistently, invest effectively, or protect yourself without a clean banking system.

Well-organized banking reduces friction. It supports better habits. It allows you to focus on decisions that actually move you forward instead of constantly fixing avoidable problems.

Just like well-maintained equipment allows you to focus on playing, organized banking allows you to focus on building wealth.

Coach's Perspective: What Would Your Coach Say?

A coach would keep this simple.

"Take care of your gear."

"Be organized."

"Details matter."

"Don't beat yourself."

Financially, that means keeping accounts simple, understanding how money flows, and using safeguards. Coaches hate preventable mistakes. Banking mistakes fall into that category.

Game Situations and Decision Points

Situation one. You get paid, but you are not sure when the funds actually clear. Do you spend immediately or wait until money is available?

Situation two. You notice a small unfamiliar charge. Do you ignore it or investigate right away?

Situation three. You keep overdrafting by accident. Do you accept fees as normal or adjust your system?

Each situation mirrors equipment mistakes. You do not blame yourself endlessly. You fix the setup so it does not keep happening.

Common Athlete Mistakes and Financial Parallels

Athletes sometimes neglect gear until it fails. Financially, that shows up as ignoring bank accounts.

Athletes sometimes overcomplicate setups. Financially, that shows up as too many accounts with no clear purpose.

Athletes sometimes ignore warnings. Financially, that shows up as overdrafts, fees, and fraud issues.

Organization fixes these issues. Not effort. Not intelligence. Organization.

Winning the Long Game

Banking basics are not exciting, but they are foundational.

A clean system reduces stress, saves money, and supports better decisions. It keeps small issues from becoming big problems. It creates confidence because you know where things stand.

Organize your equipment bag. Protect your gear. Trust the setup.

Everything else builds from there.

Athlete Takeaways

- Checking moves money, savings protects it
- Separate roles create clarity
- Understand timing to avoid errors
- Alerts prevent overdrafts and fraud
- Organized systems reduce stress

Part II: Defense, Protection, and Staying in the Game

Defense keeps you competitive even when the bats go cold.

Every softball team goes through stretches where runs are hard to come by.

The timing is off. Hits find gloves. The other pitcher is dealing. In those moments, good teams do not panic. They lean on defense. They make routine plays. They protect every out and keep the game within reach until momentum shifts.

Money works the same way.

There will be seasons where income is tight, expenses spike, or progress feels slow. When that happens, offense alone will not save you. Defense keeps you alive. Protection prevents small problems from turning into disasters. Staying in the game long enough is often what creates the next opportunity.

This section of the book focuses on protecting what you are building.

Defense in money is about risk awareness, insurance, and safeguards that absorb impact when things go wrong. It is not about fear. It is about preparation. Just like a great shortstop expects hard-hit balls, smart financial defense assumes life will not always cooperate.

Many people skip this part because it feels pessimistic or boring. Athletes know better. Defense is effort, positioning, and discipline. It wins championships quietly.

You will learn how to think about risk the way you think about matchups and situations. Not all risks are equal. Some are worth taking. Others should be avoided. Understanding the difference changes everything.

This section also addresses insurance, an area many athletes misunderstand or ignore until it is too late. Insurance is not about expecting bad things to happen. It is about limiting damage when they do. One injury should not end a season. One setback should not undo years of work.

Protection also creates confidence. When you know your bases are covered, you play freer. You take smart risks. You stay composed under pressure. Financially, the same thing happens. Defense gives you the freedom to focus on progress instead of constantly reacting to threats.

Another theme in this section is staying in the game. Financial success is often less about how fast you move forward and more about how well you avoid being knocked out. Avoiding catastrophic mistakes matters more than chasing big wins early.

Defense is not passive. It is intentional. It requires effort, awareness, and maintenance. Just like fielding drills never stop, financial protection is something you review and adjust over time.

By the end of this section, you should feel more secure and more prepared. Not invincible. Just ready. Ready to handle adversity without panic. Ready to protect momentum. Ready to keep playing even when conditions are not ideal.

When the bats go cold, defense keeps you alive. In money, protection does the same.

Chapter 6: Risk Awareness and Smart Play Calling

In softball, every pitch and every play carries risk.

A bunt can turn into an easy out or spark a rally. A steal attempt can shift momentum or shut it down instantly. A pitch painted on the corner can be a strike, or it can drift an inch and get crushed. Smart teams understand risk, not by avoiding it completely, but by choosing it intentionally.

Money works the same way.

Many athletes struggle with money not because they are reckless, but because they were never taught how to evaluate risk outside of sports. They are comfortable taking physical risks, emotional risks, and competitive risks. Financial risk feels different because the rules are unclear and the feedback is slower. You do not get instant results. You do not get a scoreboard update after every decision.

This chapter is about learning how to call smarter plays with money by understanding risk the same way you already understand the game.

Emotional Risk vs Financial Risk

Emotional risk and financial risk are not the same thing, but they often get confused.

Emotional risk is how something feels. Fear. Excitement. Pressure. Confidence. Regret. These emotions are loud, especially when money is involved. Financial risk is what actually happens to your resources over time if things go wrong.

In softball, swinging on a 3–0 pitch might feel risky emotionally. Everyone is watching. The coach might have given the take sign. But the real risk depends on the score, the inning, and your role. If you are up big early, the risk is low. If it is late in a tight game, the risk is higher.

Financial decisions work the same way.

Something can feel terrifying and still be financially reasonable. Investing during a market downturn often feels awful emotionally, but financially it may be sound if you have time. Something else can feel exciting and be financially reckless. Chasing a hot investment because everyone is talking about it feels good, but the downside risk can be significant.

Learning to separate feelings from facts is one of the most important skills in money. Emotions matter. Ignoring them entirely is unrealistic. But emotions cannot drive decisions. They provide information, not direction.

Great athletes feel pressure. They just do not let it dictate every move. Money requires the same discipline.

Time Horizon and Flexibility

Time horizon is how long you have before you need the money.

Athletes understand this instinctively. A decision in the first inning is different from a decision in the seventh. Early in the game, you have flexibility. You can experiment. You can recover from mistakes. Late in the game, you protect the lead and avoid unnecessary risks.

Financially, longer time horizons allow for more risk because there is time to recover from setbacks. Shorter time horizons require more protection because mistakes have less time to heal.

Flexibility also matters.

If you can adjust, wait, or change course, you can afford to be more aggressive. If you need money at a specific time for a down payment, tuition, or living expenses, caution matters more than potential upside.

Ignoring time horizon is like calling aggressive plays late in a close game.

It might work once, but it is rarely smart. Over time, that approach loses more games than it wins.

Understanding time horizon turns risk from something scary into something manageable.

How Risk Affects Every Money Decision

Risk is not just about investing.

It shows up in spending, debt, insurance, career decisions, and even relationships. Every financial decision carries tradeoffs. The goal is not to eliminate risk. The goal is to understand it.

Taking on debt increases risk. Sometimes that risk is worth it. Education. A manageable mortgage. Business investment. Other times it is not.

Having no savings increases risk. One unexpected expense can create a chain reaction of stress and bad decisions.

Overconcentrating investments increases risk. Putting everything into one stock, one idea, or one asset ties your future to a single outcome.

Not taking any risk at all also has consequences. Avoiding investing entirely may feel safe, but it increases the risk of falling behind long term.

Smart play calling balances these factors. Just like in softball, you do not eliminate risk from the game. You choose which risks are worth taking based on the situation.

Knowing When to Be Aggressive and When to Play It Safe

Great teams know when to push and when to protect.

Early in a season, teams experiment. Lineups shift. Strategies are tested. Late in a season, teams trust what works. They rely on fundamentals. They reduce mistakes.

The same applies to money.

Aggression makes sense when you have time, stable income, and a margin for error. Investing early and consistently is often a smart form of aggression.

Playing it safe makes sense when resources are tight, goals are close, or uncertainty is high. Protecting cash, reducing debt, and lowering volatility can be the right call.

The mistake is using the same strategy in every situation.

Some people are always aggressive, regardless of context. Others are always cautious, regardless of opportunity. Both approaches ignore situational awareness.

Smart financial decisions change as life changes.

Coach's Perspective: What Would Your Coach Say?

A coach would not overcomplicate this.

"Know the situation."

"Don't force it."

"Trust the plan."

"Play smart."

Financially, that means aligning decisions with time horizon, goals, and flexibility. It means not letting emotion override awareness. Coaches do not want players freelancing just to feel important. Investors should not either.

Game Situations and Decision Points

Situation one. You have a long time before retirement. Markets fluctuate. Do you avoid all risk because it feels uncomfortable, or do you invest with intention knowing time is on your side?

Situation two. You need money within a year. Do you chase higher returns and risk loss, or do you protect capital so the money is there when you need it?

Situation three. Markets feel volatile and everyone is talking about it. Do you react emotionally, or do you stick to the game plan you built during calm periods?

Each situation mirrors a softball decision. Context matters. The same play can be brilliant or disastrous depending on timing.

Common Athlete Mistakes and Financial Parallels

Athletes sometimes confuse aggression with intelligence. Swinging hard is not the same as swinging smart. Financially, this shows up as unnecessary risk, chasing returns, or forcing plays that do not fit the situation.

Athletes sometimes play too cautiously out of fear. They stop trusting their training. Financially, this shows up as avoiding investing entirely, keeping everything in cash, or freezing under pressure.

Athletes sometimes ignore the game situation. They try to do the same thing every inning. Financially, this shows up as poor timing, ignoring time horizon, or failing to adjust as life changes.

These mistakes are fixable with awareness. The skill already exists. It just needs to be applied to money.

Winning the Long Game

Risk is part of the game.

Avoiding it completely guarantees stagnation. Embracing it blindly guarantees mistakes. The goal is neither extreme.

Smart teams respect risk. They study it. They plan for it. They choose it intentionally based on the situation, not on emotion.

Do the same with money.

You do not need to predict outcomes. You need to make decisions that make sense given your time horizon, flexibility, and goals. Over time, that approach compounds.

Athlete Takeaways

- Risk is situational, not emotional
- Time horizon changes the right decision
- Flexibility increases your margin for error
- Aggression without context is reckless
- Smart play calling beats blind confidence

Chapter 7: Insurance Fundamentals Every Player Needs

In softball, you do not step on the field without the basics. Cleats that fit. A glove you trust. Protective gear that keeps you in the game when contact happens. You hope you never need some of it, but you would never play without it.

Insurance works the same way.

Insurance is not about expecting bad things to happen. It is about limiting damage when they do. One injury should not end a season. One accident should not derail years of progress. This chapter covers the insurance fundamentals every athlete needs to understand so setbacks stay manageable instead of catastrophic.

Health Insurance Basics

Health insurance is the most important coverage most people will ever have, and it is also one of the most confusing.

At its core, health insurance exists to share risk. You pay premiums so that when medical costs show up, you are not responsible for everything on your own. The problem is that many athletes only learn how health insurance works after they need it.

Key terms matter.

Premiums are what you pay to keep coverage active. Deductibles are what you pay out of pocket before insurance starts sharing costs. Copays and coinsurance determine how costs are split after the deductible is met. Out-of-pocket maximums cap how much you can be responsible for in a year.

Athletes understand this concept from training rooms. Some treatment is covered. Some requires approval. Some has limits. Knowing the rules ahead of time prevents surprises.

One of the biggest mistakes people make is choosing coverage based only on the monthly premium. A low premium with a high deductible may work for someone with savings and low medical needs. It can be dangerous for someone living paycheck to paycheck.

The goal is not the cheapest plan. The goal is the plan that fits your risk tolerance, health needs, and financial situation.

Auto and Renters Insurance

Auto insurance is required in most places, but minimum coverage is rarely enough.

Auto insurance protects against damage you cause, damage to your vehicle, and injuries. Liability coverage is especially important. If you cause an accident and injuries exceed your coverage, the rest can come out of your pocket.

Athletes often underestimate this risk. One accident can lead to lawsuits, wage garnishment, and long-term financial damage. Adequate liability limits protect future income, not just your car.

Renters insurance is one of the most misunderstood and underused forms of coverage.

It is inexpensive and powerful. Renters insurance protects personal belongings, provides liability coverage, and often covers temporary housing if your place becomes unlivable. Many athletes assume their landlord's insurance covers them. It does not.

Think of renters insurance like protecting everything in your locker. Gear, electronics, clothes, and personal items add up quickly. Renters insurance keeps a small incident from becoming a major setback.

Homeowners Insurance

Homeowners insurance combines property protection with liability coverage.

It covers the structure, personal belongings, and responsibility if someone is injured on your property. It also protects against events like fire, storms, and theft.

The biggest mistake homeowners make is assuming the purchase price equals the coverage needed. Rebuilding costs can differ significantly from market value. Coverage should be based on replacement cost, not what you paid.

Homeowners insurance also interacts with other parts of your financial life. Higher deductibles lower premiums but require cash reserves. Liability limits matter more as assets grow.

As life progresses, coverage should evolve. Just like equipment changes as players advance, insurance needs change with responsibility.

Deductibles, Premiums, and Coverage Limits

These three elements determine how insurance behaves.

Premiums are predictable. Deductibles are what you absorb first. Coverage limits determine how much protection you actually have.

Lower premiums usually mean higher deductibles or lower limits. Higher premiums usually mean more protection and less out-of-pocket exposure.

There is no universal right answer. The right setup balances affordability with protection. Athletes understand this tradeoff instinctively. Lightweight gear feels faster but offers less protection. Heavier gear offers more protection but requires adjustment.

The same thinking applies here.

The key is alignment. Deductibles should match available savings. Coverage limits should protect what you have and what you are building.

The Investing Concept Explained Through the Sport

Insurance does not generate returns. It preserves opportunity.

In softball, defense does not score runs, but it prevents losses. Insurance plays the same role financially. It protects your ability to keep earning, saving, and investing after setbacks.

Skipping insurance to save money is like skipping protective gear to feel faster. It works until it does not.

Coach's Perspective: What Would Your Coach Say?

A coach would keep it simple.

"Protect yourself."

"Be prepared."

"Don't take unnecessary risks."

"Availability matters."

Financially, that means having coverage in place before you need it, understanding the rules, and not cutting corners on protection.

Game Situations and Decision Points

Situation one. You choose the cheapest insurance option without understanding deductibles. A medical issue hits. Do you have the cash to cover it?

Situation two. You skip renters insurance. A fire damages your belongings. Do you replace everything out of pocket?

Situation three. You carry minimal auto liability. An accident exceeds your limits. How does that affect your future income?

Each situation mirrors a softball decision. Preparation determines outcome.

Common Athlete Mistakes and Financial Parallels

Athletes sometimes rely on luck instead of protection. Financially, that shows up as underinsuring.

Athletes sometimes avoid boring preparation. Financially, that shows up as skipping insurance reviews.

Athletes sometimes underestimate risk because nothing has happened yet. Financially, that creates exposure.

These mistakes are common and preventable.

Winning the Long Game

Insurance does not make you rich. It keeps you from getting knocked out.

It allows you to take smart risks elsewhere because your foundation is protected. It keeps bad breaks from defining your financial future.

Understand your coverage. Choose intentionally. Review it as life changes.

Defense keeps you in the game. Insurance is part of that defense.

Athlete Takeaways

- Insurance limits damage, it does not predict disaster
- Choose coverage based on risk, not just price
- Liability protects future income, not just today
- Deductibles must match your savings
- Strong defense creates long-term confidence

Chapter 8: Life, Disability, and Liability Protection

Athletes understand one simple truth. Your ability to compete matters, but your ability to stay on the field matters more.

Talent does not help if you cannot play. Preparation does not matter if one hit takes you out of the game. That is why strength training, recovery, and protective gear are taken seriously. You cannot control everything, but you can control how exposed you are.

Life, disability, and liability insurance exist for the same reason.

These forms of protection are not about pessimism. They are about responsibility. They protect income, people who depend on you, and the progress you are building. Skipping them is not confidence. It is gambling.

Term vs Permanent Life Insurance

Life insurance answers one question. If something happens to you, what happens to the people who rely on your income?

Term life insurance is simple. It covers you for a specific period of time, like 20 or 30 years. If you pass away during that term, the benefit pays out. If not, the coverage ends.

Permanent life insurance lasts for life and includes a savings component. It is more complex and more expensive.

For most athletes and young families, term insurance makes sense. It is affordable, straightforward, and designed to cover the years when responsibilities are highest. Mortgage. Kids. Income replacement.

Think of term insurance like protective gear you wear during the most physical years of competition. You need it when risk is high. You may not need it forever.

Permanent insurance can have a role in advanced planning situations, but it is often oversold and misunderstood. Complexity does not equal superiority. Fit matters more than labels.

The biggest mistake athletes make is assuming they are too young or too healthy to need life insurance. Risk does not care about age, and premiums increase as you get older. Coverage is cheapest when you are healthy and early in your career.

Disability Insurance and Income Protection

If life insurance protects others, disability insurance protects you.

Your greatest asset is not your investments. It is your ability to earn income. If that stops, everything else gets stressed.

Athletes understand this better than most. An injury that takes you out changes everything. Disability insurance exists to replace a portion of income if you cannot work due to illness or injury.

Many people assume this will never happen to them. Statistics disagree.

Short-term disability covers temporary interruptions. Long-term disability protects income for years, sometimes until retirement age. Employer plans often provide limited coverage. Individual policies add control and flexibility.

The key details matter. How much income is covered. How long benefits last. How long you wait before benefits start.

Skipping disability insurance is like refusing rehab because you feel fine today. It ignores reality.

Umbrella Liability Coverage

Umbrella insurance is about protecting your future.

It provides extra liability coverage above auto and homeowners or renters policies. Lawsuits do not care how old you are or how much you intended to risk. They care about damages.

As income grows and assets accumulate, exposure increases. One accident, one mistake, one misunderstanding can create financial consequences far beyond standard limits.

Umbrella coverage is relatively inexpensive compared to the protection it provides. It exists to catch the worst-case scenarios so they do not wipe out everything you have built.

Athletes often underestimate this risk because nothing has happened yet. That logic fails quickly when something does.

Common Insurance Mistakes Athletes Make

The most common mistake is delaying coverage.

Athletes wait because money feels tight or because insurance feels boring. The problem is that insurance is cheapest and easiest to secure before something goes wrong.

Another mistake is underestimating income value. People focus on assets and ignore future earnings. Disability and life insurance exist to protect that earning power.

Many athletes also rely entirely on employer coverage without understanding limits. Jobs change. Coverage ends. Gaps appear.

Another mistake is chasing complexity. Fancy products are not better if they do not fit your situation. Simple, well-structured protection usually works best.

Finally, athletes often fail to update coverage as life changes. New jobs. Marriage. Kids. Home ownership. Protection should evolve with responsibility.

The Investing Concept Explained Through the Sport

Protection enables offense.

In softball, strong defense allows aggressive play. Pitchers attack hitters. Fielders anticipate. Confidence increases.

Financially, protection does the same. When income and liability risks are covered, investing becomes easier. Decisions become calmer. Long-term thinking improves.

Skipping protection creates fear-based decisions. Panic replaces planning. Defense disappears.

Coach's Perspective: What Would Your Coach Say?

A coach would be direct.

"Protect yourself."

"Availability matters."

"Do not take unnecessary risks."

"Handle your business."

Financially, that means having life, disability, and liability protection in place before you need it. It means understanding coverage, not guessing.

Coaches prepare for worst-case scenarios so players can focus on execution. Money deserves the same respect.

Game Situations and Decision Points

Situation one. You have dependents but no life insurance. Something unexpected happens. Who absorbs the impact?

Situation two. You are injured or ill and cannot work for months. How long can you survive without income?

Situation three. You are involved in a serious accident. Are your liability limits enough to protect future earnings?

These are uncomfortable questions. Avoiding them does not make them go away.

Common Athlete Mistakes and Financial Parallels

Athletes sometimes rely on toughness instead of protection. Financially, that shows up as skipping insurance.

Athletes sometimes assume nothing will happen. Financially, that shows up as undercoverage.

Athletes sometimes overestimate control. Financially, that creates exposure.

Preparation corrects these patterns.

Winning the Long Game

Life, disability, and liability protection are not exciting. They are essential.

They protect people you care about. They protect income you have not earned yet. They protect progress you worked hard to build.

Championship teams plan for adversity. Smart financial plans do the same.

Protect your ability to stay in the game. Everything else depends on it.

Athlete Takeaways

- Your income is your most valuable asset
- Term insurance covers responsibility years efficiently
- Disability insurance protects your ability to earn
- Liability risk grows as income grows
- Strong protection creates freedom, not fear

Part III: Building the Offense (Investing Fundamentals)

Consistent contact wins more games than home runs.

Every softball player knows the temptation to swing big.

Home runs change games quickly. They feel powerful. They draw attention. But they are also rare, and chasing them often leads to strikeouts, pop-ups, and frustration. The best offenses are not built on hope. They are built on approach.

Money is no different.

Most people think investing is about finding the one big winner. The perfect stock. The hot trend. The next breakout opportunity. That mindset creates impatience and unnecessary risk. It ignores how real progress is actually made.

This section of the book focuses on building an offense that produces runs consistently over time.

Investing fundamentals are about understanding how markets work, how risk and return interact, and how patience compounds results. This is not about predicting the next pitch. It is about having an approach you can execute through every count and every inning.

Consistent contact in investing means regular contributions, diversification, and staying invested through ups and downs. It means letting time and compounding do the heavy lifting instead of forcing outcomes.

Athletes already understand this. Players who stay within themselves, trust their mechanics, and take what the defense gives them usually outperform those who swing for the fences every at bat. Investing rewards the same discipline.

This section will help you understand what you actually own when you invest, how different asset types behave, and why volatility is part of the game, not a sign that something is broken. You will learn why chasing hot streaks usually backfires and why boring, repeatable strategies tend to win over long seasons.

Another key theme here is process. Offense breaks down when players abandon approach under pressure. Investing breaks down when emotions take over during market swings. This section helps you build a process you can trust when conditions are not perfect.

You will also learn how investing fits into the larger game plan. Offense only works when defense is solid. Cash flow, savings, and protection make investing possible. Without that foundation, offense becomes reckless instead of productive.

By the end of this section, you should feel more confident about how investing actually works. Not because you can predict outcomes, but because you understand the mechanics. You will know what matters, what does not, and how to stay disciplined when noise increases.

Home runs are fun. Championships are built on consistency.

Build an offense you can execute every day, not one you hope works once.

Chapter 9: How Financial Markets Really Work

Softball players learn early that the game is bigger than any one at bat. You can square a ball up perfectly and still make an out. You can barely get the barrel on it and watch it drop in for a hit. Over the course of a season, luck evens out, preparation shows up, and the best teams rise. The standings usually make sense by the end, even if individual games felt unfair along the way.

Financial markets behave the same way, even though many people never learn to see them that way.

Markets are not designed to reward perfection in the short term. They reward discipline, participation, and patience over time. When you understand how markets actually work, investing becomes less intimidating and far more predictable in the ways that matter most.

How Markets Function

At their core, markets exist to connect people who want to grow capital with businesses and governments that need capital.

Companies raise money to build products, hire employees, expand operations, and innovate. Governments raise money to fund infrastructure, services, and long-term projects. Investors provide that capital in exchange for the opportunity to earn a return. That is it. Everything else is commentary layered on top.

Prices move because millions of participants are constantly updating expectations about the future. Earnings. Interest rates. Innovation. Regulation. Fear. Optimism. Confidence. Panic. When expectations change, prices respond.

This is similar to scouting reports and game plans.

If a pitcher adds a new pitch, hitters adjust. If a team changes defensive positioning, hitters respond differently. That does not mean the game is broken. It means information is being processed in real time.

Markets move every day because expectations change every day. That movement is normal. Silence would actually be more concerning than volatility.

Stocks, Bonds, and Ownership

Owning stock means owning a piece of a company.

You are not betting on a ticker symbol. You are not guessing on price movement alone. You are owning a share of a business with employees, customers, products, and cash flow. When companies grow profits over time, owners benefit. When companies struggle, owners feel that too.

That ownership mindset is critical.

Bonds are different.

Bonds are loans. When you buy a bond, you are lending money to a company or government. In return, you receive interest payments and the promise that your principal will be returned at maturity. Bonds are designed for income and stability, not explosive growth.

Softball players understand roles instinctively.

Some players drive in runs. Some stabilize the defense. Some bring leadership and consistency. All matter. A team full of sluggers with no defense collapses. A team full of defenders with no offense stagnates.

Stocks are offense. Bonds are defense. Neither works well alone.

Confusion happens when people buy stocks without understanding ownership or buy bonds without understanding purpose. When you know why each exists, portfolio construction stops feeling mysterious and starts feeling intentional.

Market Cycles and Volatility

Markets move in cycles.

Growth periods are followed by slowdowns. Bull markets give way to bear markets. Volatility increases and decreases. This is not failure. It is rhythm.

Softball seasons have the same pattern.

Teams start hot. Teams slump. Injuries happen. Confidence wavers. Momentum shifts. Teams that panic during slumps usually make things worse. Teams that stick to fundamentals often recover.

Volatility is not risk by itself. Volatility is movement. Risk is permanent loss. Confusing the two leads to bad decisions.

Seeing your account balance fluctuate feels uncomfortable. That discomfort is emotional risk. Financial risk depends on whether you are forced to act at the wrong time.

If you have time, volatility is part of the game. It is the price of participation. If you panic and sell during volatility, movement turns into permanent loss.

Athletes understand this lesson clearly. One bad inning is volatility. Walking off the field and quitting the season is permanent loss.

Long-Term Strategy vs Chasing Hot Streaks

Chasing hot streaks is the fastest way to lose discipline.

Every season has players who start hot. Every market has investments that surge. The temptation is to jump in late because it feels safer when results are visible. That is exactly when risk is often highest.

Athletes know better.

You do not change your swing because a teammate is on a hot streak. You trust your mechanics. You trust your preparation. You focus on what you can control.

Long-term investing works the same way.

Strategy beats reaction. Process beats prediction.

Markets reward patience, diversification, and consistency. They punish impatience, overconfidence, and constant tinkering. Trying to time markets perfectly is like trying to predict every pitch. You might guess right occasionally, but you will strike out often enough to lose the game.

The investors who win are not the ones who guess best. They are the ones who stay disciplined longest.

The Investing Concept Explained Through the Sport

Markets are seasons, not games.

One bad week does not define a year. One bad year does not define a career. Long-term results come from staying invested through full cycles, not from avoiding every downturn.

Ownership matters. Time matters. Discipline matters.

You do not need to win every at bat. You need to stay in the lineup long enough for results to compound.

Coach's Perspective: What Would Your Coach Say?

A coach would not overcomplicate this.

"Trust your approach."

"Stay within yourself."

"Do not chase."

"The season is long."

Financially, that means sticking to a plan that fits your goals and time horizon, not reacting to headlines, social media, or short-term noise. Coaches do not want players changing mechanics after every bad game. Investors should not either.

Game Situations and Decision Points

Situation one. Markets drop sharply. Headlines are loud. Everyone is talking. Do you panic and sell, or do you stay invested knowing downturns are part of the season?

Situation two. A hot investment dominates headlines and group chats. Do you chase it late, or do you stick to your allocation and process?

Situation three. Your portfolio feels boring. Nothing exciting is happening. Do you change things to feel active, or do you trust consistency?

Each situation mirrors a softball decision. Do you abandon mechanics under pressure, or do you stay disciplined and let the game come to you?

Common Athlete Mistakes and Financial Parallels

Athletes sometimes press when results slow. Investors chase returns when performance lags.

Athletes sometimes copy others instead of trusting training. Investors follow trends instead of plans.

Athletes sometimes confuse effort with forcing outcomes. Investors confuse activity with progress.

Awareness fixes these patterns. Discipline sustains success.

Winning the Long Game

Markets reward those who stay in the game.

You do not need to predict the future. You need a system that survives it. Understanding how markets work replaces fear with patience and confusion with confidence.

Consistent contact beats swinging for the fences.

Championship teams are built on fundamentals repeated over time. Financial success works the same way.

Athlete Takeaways

- Markets are systems, not slot machines
- Stocks are ownership, bonds are loans
- Volatility is movement, not failure
- Long-term strategy beats hot streaks
- Discipline over time wins seasons

Chapter 10: Risk, Return, and the Power of Compounding

Softball teaches a lesson that shows up in every season. You rarely win by avoiding the game, and you rarely win by swinging without control. Teams that play scared get exposed. Teams that swing wildly burn themselves out. Success lives in the balance between smart aggression and discipline.

Risk and return work the same way.

Many athletes hear the word risk and immediately think danger. Others hear return and think reward. In reality, they are inseparable. You cannot have one without the other. Every meaningful opportunity carries uncertainty, and every attempt to eliminate uncertainty comes with a cost.

The real skill is not avoiding risk or chasing return. It is understanding how much risk you are taking, why you are taking it, and how much time you have for it to work.

This chapter connects those ideas and shows why compounding rewards patience far more than talent, timing, or intensity.

Risk and Reward Tradeoffs

In softball, every decision has a tradeoff.

You can swing aggressively early in the count and try to do damage, or you can work the count and wait for your pitch. You can steal a base and gain position, or you can stay put and avoid the out. You can dive for a ball and make a highlight play, or you can play it on a hop and guarantee the out. Neither choice is always right or always wrong. Context decides.

Financial risk works the same way.

Higher potential returns usually come with more uncertainty. Lower risk usually comes with lower expected growth. That tradeoff is unavoidable. Anyone who promises high returns with no risk is selling fiction.

Athletes already understand this intuitively. You take more chances when the situation allows it. You protect the lead when the margin is thin. You do not play the same way in the first inning that you do in the seventh.

Investing decisions should follow the same logic.

The mistake is taking risks without understanding them or avoiding risk entirely out of fear. Both approaches lead to poor outcomes. Blind aggression leads to blowups. Total caution leads to stagnation.

Smart investors, like smart players, understand situational awareness.

Volatility vs Permanent Loss

One of the most important distinctions in investing is the difference between volatility and permanent loss.

Volatility is movement. Prices go up and down. Account balances fluctuate. Headlines change tone. This is normal. Markets breathe. Just like performance over a season rises and falls.

Permanent loss is different.

Permanent loss happens when money is gone and cannot recover. Selling after a panic. Investing in something you do not understand. Taking risks you cannot afford. Locking in mistakes because emotions override discipline.

Athletes see this difference clearly on the field.

A bad inning is volatility. You give up a few runs. Momentum shifts. It feels uncomfortable, but the game is still alive. A season-ending injury is permanent loss. The opportunity to recover is gone.

Confusing volatility with permanent loss leads to bad decisions.

Many people react to market volatility as if it is permanent. They pull out at the worst possible time, locking in losses that could have recovered with patience. The emotional discomfort becomes a financial mistake.

Time changes everything.

If you have time, volatility matters less. If you do not have time, protection matters more. The same market movement can be irrelevant to one investor and devastating to another depending on time horizon.

Understanding this distinction keeps you from overreacting to normal movement.

Compounding Over Time

Compounding is the most powerful force in investing, and it is also the least exciting to watch in the early stages.

Compounding means that returns build on previous returns. Growth feeds growth. Progress accelerates the longer you stay in the game. Early on, it barely looks like anything is happening. Later, it feels like momentum appears out of nowhere.

This is not magic. It is math and time working together.

Athletes understand this from training.

Early gains are slow. Strength builds gradually. Mechanics improve inch by inch. Conditioning feels endless. Then, at some point, something clicks. Performance jumps. Confidence rises. What looks like a breakthrough is actually the result of years of quiet, unglamorous work.

Money behaves the same way.

The first dollars invested do not look impressive. Progress feels slow. Account balances creep instead of surge. This is where most people quit or start changing strategies. They confuse boredom with failure.

The ones who stay disciplined benefit later when compounding accelerates. Growth becomes noticeable. Progress feels easier. That is not because they got smarter. It is because they stayed consistent.

Compounding does not reward intensity. It rewards consistency.

The Cost of Waiting

Waiting feels safe.

It feels responsible. It feels like avoiding mistakes. Many people tell themselves they will start investing later, once income is higher, debt is gone, or life feels more settled.

But waiting has a cost.

Every year you delay investing is a year compounding does not work for you. Time is the one variable you cannot replace. You can earn more income. You can adjust strategy. You can cut expenses. You cannot get years back.

Athletes see this in development all the time.

Missed reps show up later. Skipped seasons create gaps that are hard to close. Starting late does not mean failure, but it does mean working harder for the same result.

The same applies financially.

Waiting for perfect conditions rarely works because perfect conditions rarely exist. Markets are never calm for long. Life is never fully settled. There will always be reasons to delay.

Starting imperfectly beats waiting perfectly.

The Investing Concept Explained Through the Sport

Risk is like pitch selection. You do not swing at everything, but you do not take every pitch either. You choose based on count, situation, and confidence in your mechanics.

Volatility is like a slump. It feels uncomfortable. It tests confidence. But it does not define you unless you let it change your approach.

Compounding is like long-term development. It rewards patience, reps, and time in the system, not bursts of effort.

Waiting is like skipping practice. It feels harmless in the moment, but the cost shows up later when performance stalls.

Coach's Perspective: What Would Your Coach Say?

A coach would keep it simple.

"Trust the process."

"Reps matter."

"Do not panic."

"Stay locked in."

Financially, that means understanding risk instead of fearing it, staying invested when volatility shows up, and giving compounding time to work.

Great coaches preach patience because they know development cannot be rushed. Shortcuts rarely hold up over a full season.

Game Situations and Decision Points

Situation one. Markets drop and your account balance falls. Do you view it as volatility, or do you treat it like failure and abandon the plan?

Situation two. You feel behind financially and want to take a big risk to catch up. Do you force a play, or do you stick to the system that works over time?

Situation three. You are early in your career and assume you have time later. Do you start now, or do you keep waiting for the "right" moment?

Each situation mirrors a softball decision. Are you reacting emotionally, or are you executing intentionally?

Common Athlete Mistakes and Financial Parallels

Athletes sometimes press when they feel behind. They swing harder instead of trusting mechanics. Investors chase risk to make up ground.

Athletes sometimes quit mentally during slumps. Investors sell during downturns and lock in losses.

Athletes sometimes underestimate long-term development. Investors underestimate the power of compounding and overestimate short-term moves.

These mistakes are common. They are also correctable.

Winning the Long Game

Risk is not the enemy. Ignorance is.

Volatility is not failure. Panic is.

Compounding is not exciting. It is effective.

The long game rewards athletes who stay disciplined, trust their training, and give the process time to work. Money does the same.

You do not need to swing harder. You do not need to be perfect. You need to stay in the game long enough for the work to matter.

Athlete Takeaways

- Risk and reward are always linked
- Volatility is movement, not permanent loss
- Compounding rewards patience and reps
- Waiting costs time you cannot replace
- Stay disciplined and trust the long season

Chapter 11: Stocks Without the Highlight Reel

Stocks get marketed like highlight reels.

Big wins. Fast gains. Overnight success stories. Tickers flashing across screens. It makes investing feel like a sport built on moments instead of seasons. That framing is wrong, and it causes athletes to approach stocks the same way undisciplined hitters approach at bats. Swinging for something exciting instead of executing an approach.

Owning stocks is not about highlights.

It is about ownership, patience, and letting the game play out over time.

When athletes struggle with stocks, it is rarely because they lack intelligence. It is because the way stocks are talked about encourages bad habits. Chasing excitement. Overreacting to short-term results. Abandoning fundamentals when things feel slow or uncomfortable.

This chapter resets that perspective.

What Owning Stock Actually Means

When you buy a stock, you are not making a prediction.

You are buying ownership.

You own a piece of a real business. That business has employees, customers, expenses, profits, competitors, and long-term goals. It operates every day whether the stock price moves up, down, or sideways. If the company grows earnings over time, owners benefit. If it struggles, owners feel that too.

This is no different than being part of a team.

You are tied to the overall performance, not just one play. Some games go well. Others do not. Some seasons are strong. Others involve rebuilding. What matters is whether the organization is moving forward over time.

Problems arise when people forget ownership and focus only on price.

Price moves daily. Sometimes wildly. Business value usually changes more slowly. Confusing the two leads to emotional decisions. People panic when prices fall even if the business is stable. People chase when prices rise even if the business fundamentals have not changed.

Athletes understand this difference instinctively.

One bad game does not define a season. One great game does not guarantee anything either. Coaches evaluate patterns, not highlights. Stocks deserve the same perspective.

When you own stock, you are betting on time, execution, and discipline, not moments.

Growth vs Value Investing

Growth and value investing are often framed as opposing strategies. One is exciting. The other is boring. One is future-focused. The other is conservative.

In reality, they are just different ways of participating in ownership.

Growth investing focuses on companies expected to grow faster than average. These businesses often reinvest profits into expansion, innovation, and market share. They may not generate much current income because they are focused on future potential. Returns come primarily from growth over time.

Value investing focuses on companies that appear underpriced relative to their fundamentals. These businesses may be mature, temporarily out of favor, or misunderstood by the market. They often generate steady cash flow and may return profits to shareholders.

Think of this like roster construction.

Growth players are the young athletes with upside. High ceiling. Big potential. They might develop into stars, but there is volatility. Not every prospect pans out.

Value players are the veterans. Reliable. Steady. They may not fill highlight reels, but they show up every day and contribute.

Good teams need both.

A portfolio built entirely on growth can feel exciting, but it can also be unstable and emotionally taxing. A portfolio built entirely on value can feel steady, but it may struggle to keep pace over time. Balance matters.

The mistake is believing one style always wins.

Markets rotate. Sometimes growth leads. Sometimes value leads. Chasing whichever style is hot usually results in buying high and selling low. Discipline means holding both and letting cycles work themselves out.

Dividends and Total Return

Dividends are cash payments companies make to shareholders.

They are part of the return, not a bonus.

Some investors focus too heavily on dividends and ignore the bigger picture. Others ignore dividends entirely and chase price appreciation. Both approaches miss the point.

What matters is total return.

Total return includes price growth plus dividends over time.

In softball terms, runs matter, not how they are scored. A home run and three singles count the same. What matters is putting runs on the board consistently.

Dividends can provide stability and income. They can smooth returns during volatile periods. They can be reinvested to compound growth over time. But dividends alone do not make an investment good or bad.

Context matters.

A company cutting dividends is not automatically broken. A company paying high dividends is not automatically safe. High dividends can sometimes signal risk if they are unsustainable.

Focusing on total return keeps attention where it belongs: long-term progress, not one feature.

Common Investing Myths

Myths spread quickly when fundamentals are skipped.

One myth is that investing in stocks is gambling.

Gambling relies on chance without ownership or edge. Investing relies on ownership, diversification, and time. They are not the same. The presence of uncertainty does not make something gambling. The lack of process does.

Another myth is that you need to be an expert to invest.

You do not.

You need discipline, a system, and the ability to stick with it. Athletes succeed because they execute fundamentals consistently, not because they reinvent the game every season.

Another myth is that you should only invest when things feel safe.

Markets rarely feel safe at the best times to invest. Comfort usually arrives after prices have already risen. Fear often shows up when opportunity is greatest.

Another myth is that activity equals progress.

Trading frequently feels productive. It gives the illusion of control. In reality, excessive activity often reduces returns through poor timing, taxes, and emotional mistakes.

Athletes know this lesson well.

Extra swings outside your approach rarely help. They usually hurt. Doing less, but doing it well, often produces better results.

The Investing Concept Explained Through the Sport

Stocks are long seasons, not single games.

Ownership matters more than daily results. Development matters more than moments. Time matters more than timing.

Growth stocks are players developing upside. Value stocks are steady contributors. Dividends are runs scored quietly. Total return is the final score at the end of the season.

You win by staying invested, diversified, and disciplined, not by chasing highlights.

Coach's Perspective: What Would Your Coach Say?

A coach would be clear and direct.

"Trust your approach."

"Do not chase."

"Stay within yourself."

"Play the long game."

Financially, that means understanding what you own, why you own it, and how it fits into the overall plan. Coaches do not want players changing swings mid-season because of one bad week. Investors should not either.

Game Situations and Decision Points

Situation one. A stock you own is down, but the business fundamentals are intact. Do you panic and sell, or do you stay disciplined and review the long-term plan?

Situation two. A hot stock dominates headlines and group chats. Everyone is talking about it. Do you chase it late, or do you stick to your allocation?

Situation three. Your portfolio feels boring. Nothing exciting is happening. Do you change things to feel active, or do you trust consistency?

Each situation mirrors a softball moment. Emotion pushes one direction. Discipline points another.

Common Athlete Mistakes and Financial Parallels

Athletes sometimes try to do too much instead of doing the right things well. Investors overtrade instead of staying disciplined.

Athletes sometimes copy others instead of trusting training. Investors chase trends instead of plans.

Athletes sometimes confuse effort with forcing results. Investors mistake activity for progress.

These mistakes fade when fundamentals are respected and systems are trusted.

Winning the Long Game

Stocks reward ownership, patience, and time.

You do not need to predict which stock will be next on the highlight reel. You need exposure to businesses that grow over time and the discipline to stay invested through full cycles.

Ignore the noise. Focus on execution.

Championships are not built on highlights. They are built on consistency, fundamentals, and staying in the game long enough for the work to matter.

Athlete Takeaways

- Owning stock means owning a business
- Growth and value both have roles
- Total return matters more than headlines
- Activity is not the same as progress
- Trust your approach and stay disciplined

Chapter 12: Bonds and Playing Solid Defense

Every championship team has players who steady the game. They make routine plays. They communicate constantly. They position themselves correctly. They do not panic when momentum shifts. They may not fill highlight reels or get the loudest cheers, but coaches trust them in tight moments because they prevent small problems from becoming big ones.

That is exactly the role bonds play in a portfolio.

Bonds are not about excitement. They are about stability, predictability, and defense. They rarely get talked about with enthusiasm, which is precisely why many athletes misunderstand or ignore them. But just like defense in softball, bonds quietly shape outcomes over full seasons.

How Bonds Work

A bond is a loan.

When you buy a bond, you are lending money to a government or a company. In exchange, the borrower agrees to pay you interest and return your principal at a specified date, called maturity.

That is the entire structure. No mystery. No hype.

Bonds differ from stocks because you are not buying ownership. You are not sharing in upside growth. You are buying an obligation. The borrower owes you interest and repayment.

Athletes understand this difference instinctively.

Some players are asked to generate offense. Others are asked to limit damage. Bonds exist to limit damage. They are designed to be predictable, not explosive.

This does not make bonds inferior. It makes them purposeful.

Interest Rate and Credit Risk

Two main risks affect bonds, and understanding them helps remove fear and confusion.

The first is interest rate risk.

When interest rates rise, existing bond prices generally fall. When interest rates fall, existing bond prices tend to rise. This happens because newer bonds are issued with different rates, making older ones more or less attractive by comparison.

Longer-term bonds are more sensitive to these changes than shorter-term bonds. That does not make them bad. It just means they behave differently.

The second risk is credit risk.

Credit risk is the possibility that the borrower cannot repay the loan. Government bonds, particularly those issued by stable governments, tend to have lower credit risk. Corporate bonds vary widely depending on the financial health of the company issuing them.

Neither risk is inherently bad.

They simply need to be understood and managed.

Athletes think about matchups the same way.

Some pitchers throw harder but miss spots. Some hitters swing big but strike out more. Higher upside usually comes with higher risk. Lower risk usually comes with lower reward. The tradeoff never disappears.

Higher bond yields usually come with higher credit or interest rate risk. Lower yields usually come with greater stability. The key is knowing which role each bond plays in the overall strategy.

When Bonds Make Sense

Bonds make sense when stability matters.

They provide income. They reduce volatility. They act as shock absorbers when stock markets become unpredictable. They help smooth returns over time and reduce the emotional pressure that leads to bad decisions.

Bonds often become more important as time horizon shortens.

If you are far from your goal, you can tolerate more movement. If you are close to needing the money, protecting capital matters more than chasing growth. Bonds help shift that balance.

Bonds also help investors stay disciplined.

When markets decline, portfolios with some bond exposure tend to experience smaller swings. That cushioning effect reduces panic and helps investors stay invested instead of making emotional exits.

Athletes understand this role well.

Defense does not score runs, but it keeps the game within reach. Strong defense buys time for offense to work. Bonds do the same for portfolios.

Stability in a Diversified Portfolio

Diversification is about balance, not perfection.

A portfolio built entirely on offense is fragile. It may perform well when conditions are ideal, but it struggles when momentum shifts. A portfolio built entirely on defense stagnates. It avoids damage but lacks growth.

The right mix depends on goals, time horizon, income stability, and personal comfort with risk.

Bonds add ballast.

They smooth the ride. They reduce drawdowns. They create psychological stability as much as financial stability. That last part matters more than most people admit.

Investors who cannot sleep at night make bad decisions. They abandon plans at the worst moments. Bonds help reduce the emotional swings that lead to permanent mistakes.

In softball terms, calm defenders keep the entire team composed. Chaos spreads when stability disappears.

The Investing Concept Explained Through the Sport

Bonds are defense.

They limit damage. They create structure. They provide reliability when conditions are unpredictable. They do not win games by themselves, but they help teams survive rough stretches.

Strong defense allows offense to stay aggressive.

Strong bond allocation allows stock exposure to stay intact.

When investors remove bonds entirely, they often end up reducing stock exposure later during downturns because the emotional stress becomes too high. Bonds help prevent that mistake.

Coach's Perspective: What Would Your Coach Say?

A coach would not glamorize this role.

"Make the routine play."

"Stay steady."

"Do not get rattled."

"Protect the lead."

Financially, that means using bonds to manage risk, not eliminate it. Coaches do not remove offense because defense matters. They balance both.

Good coaches know games are lost more often by mistakes than by lack of highlights. Bonds help prevent financial mistakes.

Game Situations and Decision Points

Situation one. Markets are volatile and headlines are loud. Your portfolio feels uncomfortable. Do you sell stocks in panic, or do you lean on diversification to ride it out?

Situation two. You are nearing a major goal like a home purchase, tuition payment, or retirement. Do you stay aggressive, or do you shift toward protection?

Situation three. You avoid bonds because they seem boring and low return. Do you reconsider their role in stability and discipline?

Each situation mirrors a defensive decision on the field. Do you rush the throw, or do you stay composed and secure the out?

Common Athlete Mistakes and Financial Parallels

Athletes sometimes undervalue defense because it lacks flash. Investors ignore bonds for the same reason.

Athletes sometimes chase highlights at the expense of fundamentals. Investors chase returns without protection.

Athletes sometimes panic when momentum shifts. Investors sell during downturns and lock in losses.

Discipline corrects these patterns. Systems reinforce them.

Defense is not about fear. It is about preparation.

Winning the Long Game

Bonds will never steal the spotlight.

They will not dominate conversations or social media. They will quietly do their job. They will reduce stress. They will help you stay invested when conditions are tough.

Championship teams respect defense.

Smart investors do too.

You do not need bonds to be exciting. You need them to be dependable. Over full seasons and full careers, that dependability creates room for offense to do its work.

Athlete Takeaways

- Bonds are loans, not ownership
- Stability matters as much as growth
- Risk and yield are always linked
- Defense keeps you in the game
- Balance offense with protection

Chapter 13: Funds, ETFs, and Team-Based Investing

No softball team wins with one player.

Even the best hitter fails most of the time. Even the best pitcher needs defense behind them. Even the most talented roster collapses without depth, defined roles, and trust in the system. Championships are built when everyone contributes and no single player has to carry the entire load.

Investing works the same way.

Trying to win financially by picking one stock, one idea, or one "can't miss" opportunity puts too much pressure on a single outcome. Team-based investing spreads responsibility across many players so one mistake, one injury, or one slump does not derail the entire season.

That is why mutual funds and ETFs exist.

They allow you to own many companies at once, reduce risk, and stay disciplined without needing to scout, analyze, and monitor every individual stock on your own.

Mutual Funds vs ETFs

Mutual funds and ETFs both pool money from many investors to buy a collection of investments. When you invest in one, you are instantly diversified across dozens, hundreds, or even thousands of holdings.

The difference is how they operate.

Mutual funds are priced once per day after markets close. When you buy or sell, you do so at the end-of-day price. You do not see intraday movement, and you cannot trade in real time.

ETFs trade throughout the day like stocks. Prices move continuously while markets are open. You can buy and sell at different prices during the day.

For long-term investors, this difference usually matters far less than people think.

What matters more is what the fund owns, how diversified it is, how tax-efficient it is, and how much it costs. Obsessing over intraday pricing is like obsessing over warmup routines instead of actual preparation.

Athletes understand this concept clearly.

Some teams practice in the morning. Others practice in the afternoon. The schedule matters less than the quality of reps, consistency, and execution. Mutual funds and ETFs are tools. The outcome depends on how they are used.

Index vs Active Strategies

Index funds aim to match the performance of a specific market or segment.

They do not try to beat the market. They simply participate in it. If the market grows, index investors grow with it. If the market struggles, index investors experience that too.

Active funds try to outperform.

Managers select specific investments, adjust allocations, and attempt to add value through decisions. Sometimes they succeed. Often they do not, especially after fees and taxes are considered.

Index investing is like running a disciplined system offense.

It may not produce constant highlights, but it works consistently. It relies on structure, repetition, and efficiency. You know what you are getting.

Active investing is like calling more complex plays.

When it works, it looks impressive. When it fails, it fails loudly. Active strategies require skill, timing, discipline, and the ability to stick with them through underperformance.

Most athletes benefit from index strategies because they are simple, diversified, and reliable. They reduce the urge to overreact. Active strategies can have a role, but they should be intentional, limited, and understood.

The mistake is chasing active performance after it already happened. That is like adding a player after their breakout season and expecting the same results without context.

Fees and Expense Ratios

Fees matter more than most people realize.

Every mutual fund and ETF charges an expense ratio. This is the cost of running the fund, expressed as a percentage and deducted directly from returns. You never see a bill. The cost just quietly reduces performance.

A small difference in fees may not feel significant in one year. Over decades, it can create a massive gap in outcomes.

Athletes understand this from conditioning.

Small habits repeated daily produce big differences over seasons. Skipped warmups. Poor recovery. Lazy reps. None feel dramatic in the moment, but they add up.

Fees work the same way.

Lower fees do not guarantee better performance, but higher fees guarantee a heavier burden. Controlling what you can control is one of the simplest advantages investors have.

You cannot control markets. You can control costs.

Diversification Without Complexity

Diversification is protection.

Owning one stock is like relying on one player to win every game. It might work occasionally. It might even work for a stretch. But it is fragile.

Funds and ETFs allow you to diversify across companies, industries, and regions with minimal effort. One investment can represent hundreds or thousands of businesses. When one struggles, others may succeed.

This reduces risk without requiring constant decisions.

Complexity is not a requirement for success.

In fact, complexity often breaks down under pressure. The more moving parts you have, the more likely something goes wrong. Simple systems are easier to understand, easier to stick with, and easier to maintain when emotions run high.

Athletes know this lesson well.

The best teams execute simple things extremely well. They do not overcomplicate under pressure. Investing works the same way.

The Investing Concept Explained Through the Sport

Funds and ETFs are team rosters.

Index funds are balanced lineups designed to compete every day. Active funds are specialized strategies that may be deployed selectively. Fees are conditioning costs that affect endurance over the season. Diversification keeps the team competitive through ups and downs.

You do not win championships by chasing stars alone.

You win by building depth, defining roles, and trusting the system.

Coach's Perspective: What Would Your Coach Say?

A coach would not make this complicated.

"Trust the system."

"Play your role."

"Depth wins seasons."

"Do not overcomplicate it."

Financially, that means using funds and ETFs to stay diversified and disciplined without constant tinkering. Coaches do not redesign the playbook every game. Investors should not redesign portfolios every market move.

Game Situations and Decision Points

Situation one. You feel tempted to pick individual stocks because they seem more exciting. Do you rely on one player, or do you build a team?

Situation two. A fund has flashy recent performance but high fees. Do you chase results, or do you evaluate fundamentals?

Situation three. Your portfolio feels boring and steady. Do you change it to feel active, or do you trust diversification and discipline?

Each situation mirrors team decisions. Ego pushes one direction. Systems pull another.

Common Athlete Mistakes and Financial Parallels

Athletes sometimes rely too heavily on star players. Investors chase individual stocks.

Athletes sometimes ignore conditioning until injuries pile up. Investors ignore fees until returns disappoint.

Athletes sometimes overthink instead of executing basics. Investors add unnecessary complexity.

Simple fixes prevent these mistakes.

Build depth. Control costs. Trust preparation.

Winning the Long Game

Team-based investing works because it spreads risk, reduces emotion, and rewards patience.

You do not need to scout every company. You do not need to predict which stock will be next to surge. You need exposure to the system and the discipline to stay invested through full seasons and cycles.

Depth wins championships.

It wins financially too.

Athlete Takeaways

- Funds spread risk across a team
- Index strategies reward discipline
- Fees compound against you
- Diversification reduces pressure
- Simple systems survive long seasons

Chapter 14: Real Estate and Alternative Plays

Every softball player learns early that not every play looks the same. Sometimes you take the sure out. Sometimes you turn two. Sometimes you hold the runner and live to fight the next pitch. The right decision depends on the situation, not on ego, excitement, or what looks impressive in the moment.

Real estate and alternative investments work the same way.

They can be powerful tools when used correctly. They can also create stress, complexity, and regret when forced into the wrong situation. This chapter is about understanding the role these investments can play without overcomplicating the game plan.

Renting vs Owning

Renting and owning are often framed as a moral decision.

Rent is bad. Ownership is good. That framing misses reality.

Renting buys flexibility. Owning builds long-term equity and stability. Neither is always right.

Athletes understand this instinctively. Early in a career, flexibility matters. You might relocate for school, a job, or opportunity. Income may be uneven. Life may change quickly. Renting keeps options open and limits long-term commitments.

Later, when income stabilizes and roots are set, ownership can make more sense. You trade flexibility for control and long-term predictability.

Owning a home is not just an investment decision. It is a lifestyle choice.

Maintenance. Repairs. Property taxes. Insurance. Time. These costs are real, even if they are not always obvious upfront. Buying too early or stretching too far financially can create stress instead of security.

Athletes have seen this before. Taking on responsibility before you are ready can hurt development. Timing matters.

The right decision depends on income stability, time horizon, location, and personal goals. There is no universal rule. Anyone telling you there is one is oversimplifying the game.

REITs and Indirect Ownership

Real estate investment trusts, or REITs, allow investors to own real estate indirectly.

Instead of buying, managing, and maintaining properties yourself, you own shares in companies that own and operate real estate. These can include apartments, office buildings, warehouses, data centers, and retail spaces.

REITs provide three things many athletes value.

Diversification. Liquidity. Simplicity.

They allow exposure to real estate without requiring hands-on management. They trade like stocks, meaning they can be bought and sold easily. Many pay regular income.

Think of REITs like being part of a deep roster rather than running the entire program yourself. You benefit from professional management and scale without having to call every play.

Direct ownership offers more control and potential tax benefits, but it also requires time, expertise, and tolerance for headaches. Tenants. Repairs. Vacancies. Market shifts. These are part of the deal.

Indirect ownership simplifies participation. It is not better or worse by default. It is different.

The mistake is assuming real estate only counts if you personally own the building. Exposure matters more than ego.

Alternatives Like Commodities and Private Investments

Alternative investments include things like commodities, private equity, private credit, hedge strategies, and other non-traditional assets.

These investments often behave differently than stocks and bonds. That difference can improve diversification. It can also introduce complexity, higher fees, and limited transparency.

Athletes should be cautious here.

Complexity does not equal sophistication.

Many alternative investments are marketed aggressively. High returns. Exclusive access. Limited availability. These phrases trigger the same instincts as highlight reels and insider opportunities.

Understanding how returns are generated matters. Understanding fee structures matters. Understanding when and how you can access your money matters.

Many alternatives are illiquid. Your money may be locked up for years. That is not inherently bad, but it increases risk if it does not fit your overall situation.

Alternatives can play a role for some investors, usually after a solid foundation is built. They are rarely a starting point and almost never a substitute for fundamentals.

Athletes do not run trick plays before mastering basics. Investing should follow the same logic.

Liquidity and Risk Considerations

Liquidity is how quickly you can turn an investment into cash without significant loss.

Stocks and bonds are liquid. You can sell them quickly and know roughly what you will receive. Real estate and many alternatives are not.

Illiquidity increases risk in two important ways.

First, it limits flexibility. If you need money unexpectedly, you may not be able to access it easily.

Second, it increases emotional stress. Feeling trapped financially leads to poor decisions elsewhere.

Athletes who invest heavily in illiquid assets without adequate cash reserves often feel pressure they did not anticipate. That pressure shows up in stress, second-guessing, and rushed decisions.

Risk is not just about losing money.

It is about losing flexibility.

Before investing in real estate or alternatives, ask simple questions.

How long is my money tied up?

What happens if I need cash?

Do I understand the risks and fees?

How does this fit with everything else I own?

If answers are unclear, caution is warranted. There is no rush to add complexity.

The Investing Concept Explained Through the Sport

Real estate and alternative investments are situational plays.

They are not everyday swings. They are not automatic decisions. They are tools used when the situation calls for them.

Smart teams know when to stick with fundamentals and when to add wrinkles. They do not force complexity just to feel advanced.

In investing, fundamentals come first. Cash flow. Diversification. Liquidity. Discipline. Real estate and alternatives layer on top of that foundation when appropriate.

Coach's Perspective: What Would Your Coach Say?

A coach would slow this down.

"Know the situation."

"Do not force it."

"Understand your role."

"Protect flexibility."

Financially, that means not rushing into complex investments without understanding tradeoffs. Coaches do not call trick plays every inning. Investors should not either.

The goal is not to look smart. It is to make decisions that work under pressure.

Game Situations and Decision Points

Situation one. You feel pressure to buy a home because everyone else is. Do you evaluate whether it fits your timeline and income, or do you follow noise?

Situation two. An alternative investment promises high returns but limits access to your money for years. Do you fully understand the risks and tradeoffs?

Situation three. You want exposure to real estate but do not want the hassle of management. Do you consider indirect options like REITs?

Each situation mirrors a softball decision. Do you rush the play because it looks exciting, or do you make the play that fits the moment?

Common Athlete Mistakes and Financial Parallels

Athletes sometimes chase what others are doing instead of trusting development. Investors follow real estate hype without evaluating fit.

Athletes sometimes overestimate control. Investors underestimate the complexity of managing property or alternative investments.

Athletes sometimes ignore recovery and flexibility. Investors ignore liquidity until it becomes a problem.

These patterns create problems when fundamentals are skipped.

Winning the Long Game

Real estate and alternative investments can be valuable tools. They are not shortcuts.

They work best when layered onto a strong foundation, not used to replace it. Flexibility, clarity, and discipline matter more than excitement.

You do not need every investment. You need the right ones for your situation.

Make the play that fits the moment. Trust the fundamentals. Protect flexibility so you can stay in the game long enough to win.

Athlete Takeaways

- Renting buys flexibility, owning builds equity
- REITs offer real estate exposure without management
- Alternatives add complexity and risk
- Liquidity matters more than excitement
- Fit the play to the situation

Part IV: Managing the Game and Making Adjustments

Smart teams adjust without panicking.

Every softball game changes as it unfolds.

Pitchers tire. Hitters adjust. Weather shifts. Momentum swings. The teams that stay composed and make smart adjustments gain an edge. The teams that panic, overcorrect, or abandon their plan usually beat themselves.

Money behaves the same way.

No financial plan survives untouched. Careers change. Income rises and falls. Goals evolve. Markets move. The difference between long-term success and frustration is not avoiding change, but managing it well.

This section of the book focuses on how to manage your financial game once the foundation is in place.

Adjustments are part of the process. Reviewing accounts, rebalancing investments, and updating strategies are signs of discipline, not failure. Just like in softball, adjustments should be intentional, measured, and based on information, not emotion.

One of the biggest mistakes athletes make financially is confusing movement with progress. Constant tinkering feels productive, but it often leads to worse outcomes. Smart teams trust their system and adjust only when the situation truly calls for it.

This section will help you understand when to make changes and when to stay put. You will learn how to evaluate performance without overreacting, how to handle life transitions without derailing momentum, and how to stay disciplined when noise increases.

Managing the game also means understanding your role at different stages of life. Early innings allow experimentation. Late innings require protection. The same plan does not work forever, and adjusting does not mean starting over.

You will also learn how mental discipline affects financial outcomes. Pressure, comparison, and fear all influence decisions. Managing those forces is just as important as managing numbers.

By the end of this section, you should feel more confident making changes without abandoning your plan. You will understand that adjustments are part of winning, not signs of weakness.

Stay composed. Read the situation. Make the smart play.

That is how smart teams manage the game.

Chapter 15: Asset Allocation and Lineup Balance

Every great softball coach cares about lineup balance.

You do not stack nine hitters with the same strengths and weaknesses and expect consistent results. You mix speed and power. You balance right-handed and left-handed bats. You build depth so one slump does not sink the team.

Asset allocation works the same way.

It is not about finding the perfect investment. It is about how different pieces work together. The mix matters more than any single position.

Stocks, Bonds, and Cash Balance

Stocks, bonds, and cash each play a role.

Stocks drive growth. They create long-term upside and are the engine of progress.

Bonds provide stability. They reduce volatility and help smooth the ride when markets get rough.

Cash provides flexibility. It covers short-term needs, emergencies, and opportunities.

Too much stock exposure creates stress and volatility. Too much bond or cash exposure creates stagnation. Balance is what allows a portfolio to function through different conditions.

Athletes understand this from lineup construction. Too much power and no speed limits options. Too much defense and no offense limits scoring. Balance creates adaptability.

Domestic vs International Exposure

Many investors concentrate everything in their home market because it feels familiar.

Familiar does not always mean safer.

Domestic and international markets move differently over time. Different economies, currencies, and growth patterns create diversification benefits. When one region struggles, another may lead.

This is like recruiting from one region only. It limits perspective and depth. Broader exposure increases resilience.

International investing does not mean abandoning domestic strength. It means complementing it.

Diversification Principles

Diversification is about reducing reliance on any one outcome.

It spreads risk across companies, industries, and regions. It does not eliminate risk, but it makes outcomes more predictable.

Athletes understand this intuitively. Depth charts exist for a reason. Injuries happen. Slumps happen. Diversification keeps the team competitive.

Over-diversification can dilute effectiveness. Under-diversification creates fragility. The goal is thoughtful balance.

Career-Stage Allocation

Asset allocation should evolve over time.

Early in your career, time is your biggest advantage. Longer horizons allow more stock exposure and higher volatility.

Mid-career, priorities shift. Income stabilizes. Goals multiply. Balance becomes more important.

Later in life, protecting what you have built matters more than aggressive growth. Bonds and cash play larger roles.

Using the same allocation forever ignores reality. Adjusting based on career stage is not timing the market. It is matching strategy to situation.

The Investing Concept Explained Through the Sport

Asset allocation is lineup construction.

Stocks are power hitters. Bonds are steady defenders. Cash is the bench that gives flexibility.

Domestic and international exposure create balance. Career stage determines strategy.

Winning lineups evolve as the season progresses.

Coach's Perspective: What Would Your Coach Say?

"Balance the lineup."

"Know your personnel."

"Do not overreact."

"Adjust with purpose."

Financially, that means building an allocation that fits your goals and time horizon, not chasing whatever is hot.

Game Situations and Decision Points

Situation one. Markets rise and stocks dominate returns. Do you rebalance or let imbalance grow?

Situation two. You feel nervous about volatility. Do you eliminate stocks or adjust proportionally?

Situation three. Your career stage changes. Do you update your allocation or ignore reality?

Each situation mirrors lineup decisions. Balance matters.

Common Athlete Mistakes and Financial Parallels

Athletes sometimes overload strengths. Investors overconcentrate.

Athletes sometimes avoid change. Investors stick with outdated allocations.

Athletes sometimes chase momentum. Investors chase performance.

These patterns are correctable with discipline.

Winning the Long Game

Asset allocation determines how your portfolio behaves.

It shapes risk. It influences returns. It impacts emotional discipline.

You do not win seasons with an unbalanced lineup. You do not build wealth with an unbalanced portfolio.

Build a lineup that fits the season you are in.

Athlete Takeaways

- Allocation matters more than individual picks
- Balance offense, defense, and flexibility
- Diversification protects against slumps
- Career stage should drive strategy
- Adjust intentionally, not emotionally

Chapter 16: Buying, Holding, and Trusting the Game Plan

At some point, every team reaches a moment where preparation turns into execution.

The plan has been installed. Reps have been taken. Film has been reviewed. Coaches have said everything they can say. Now the game starts, and the only thing left to do is trust what you have built. The teams that succeed are not the ones that reinvent everything mid-game. They are the ones that execute the plan and stay composed when things get noisy.

Investing works the same way.

Most people fail at investing not because they lack information, but because they struggle with execution. Buying, holding, and trusting the game plan sounds simple. In practice, it is where discipline gets tested and emotions show up.

This chapter is about moving from theory to action, and then having the patience to let that action work.

Opening and Funding Accounts

Before you can invest, you need the right accounts.

This step feels administrative, which is why many people rush it or avoid it entirely. That is a mistake. Account type affects taxes, flexibility, and long-term outcomes. Getting this right early makes everything else easier.

Retirement accounts, brokerage accounts, and employer plans all serve different purposes. Retirement accounts offer tax advantages but limit access. Brokerage accounts offer flexibility but fewer tax benefits. Employer plans often include matching contributions that act like free money.

The goal is not to open everything at once.

The goal is to open the accounts that fit your current situation, income, and goals. As life changes, accounts can be added or adjusted. Investing is not an all-or-nothing decision.

Funding accounts matters just as much as opening them.

An unfunded account does nothing. A perfectly selected investment with no money behind it produces no results. Consistent contributions matter far more than perfect timing.

Athletes understand this immediately.

Signing up for a training program does not make you stronger. Showing up consistently does. Miss enough sessions, and progress stalls. The same is true financially.

Automation is the most powerful tool here.

When contributions happen automatically, discipline replaces willpower. You do not have to decide every month. The system does the work. This is how good intentions turn into consistent results.

Market Orders vs Limit Orders

Market orders and limit orders are tools. Knowing the difference prevents mistakes, but obsessing over them can become a distraction.

A market order buys or sells immediately at the current price. A limit order sets a specific price and waits until that price is available.

For long-term investors, this distinction often matters far less than people think.

If you are investing regularly and planning to hold for years or decades, small price differences at entry rarely change outcomes in a meaningful way. What matters is participation and consistency.

Obsessing over perfect entry points is often hesitation disguised as intelligence.

Athletes recognize this pattern. Overthinking slows reaction. Hesitation leads to late swings. Trusting mechanics speeds execution.

Use the tools appropriately, but do not let mechanics replace discipline. You do not win by waiting for perfect conditions. You win by executing when the pitch comes.

Buy-and-Hold Discipline

Buy-and-hold is often misunderstood.

It is not passive. It is intentional.

Buy-and-hold means you buy investments that fit your plan and hold them through normal ups and downs. It does not mean ignoring reality or refusing to adjust when life changes. It means not reacting to every headline, market move, or emotional impulse.

Athletes know this lesson well.

You do not abandon your swing because of one bad series. You do not scrap your training because of one slump. You trust the work. You make small, thoughtful adjustments when necessary, but you do not start over every week.

Buy-and-hold works because markets reward time.

Compounding requires staying invested. Selling breaks the chain. Every time you jump in and out, you reset progress and introduce timing risk.

The hardest part of investing is not buying.

It is holding when things feel uncomfortable. That discomfort is where discipline matters most.

Avoiding Emotional Decisions

Emotions are the biggest threat to investment success.

Fear shows up during market drops. Greed shows up during rallies. Comparison shows up when others appear to be winning faster. Confidence turns into overconfidence. Anxiety turns into paralysis.

None of these emotions are useful for decision-making.

Athletes are trained to manage emotion under pressure.

Slow the game down. Control your breathing. Focus on the next pitch, not the last mistake or the scoreboard. Investing requires the same approach.

If a financial decision feels urgent, it usually deserves a pause.

Urgency is often emotional, not strategic. Real opportunities rarely disappear overnight. Panic decisions usually cause more damage than missed opportunities.

Systems help here.

Automatic investing removes timing decisions. Rebalancing schedules provide structure. Written plans clarify intent before emotions show up. These systems act like coaches on the sideline, reminding you what matters when adrenaline spikes.

You cannot eliminate emotion. You can prevent it from running the game.

The Investing Concept Explained Through the Sport

Buying is showing up prepared.

Holding is trusting your training.

Avoiding emotional decisions is staying composed in tight moments.

You do not win by changing the plan every inning. You win by executing it consistently, especially when conditions are difficult.

Great teams look boring when they are winning the right way. Their discipline does not make headlines, but it produces results.

Investing success often looks the same.

Coach's Perspective: What Would Your Coach Say?

A coach would not overcomplicate this.

"Trust the plan."

"Stay locked in."

"Do not flinch."

"Next play."

Financially, that means following through on your strategy even when markets test your confidence. Coaches do not want players freelancing under pressure. Investors should not either.

Execution beats improvisation over long seasons.

Game Situations and Decision Points

Situation one. Markets drop sharply and your account balance falls. Do you sell to stop the emotional discomfort, or do you hold and allow time to work?

Situation two. A strong rally makes investing feel easy. Everyone is confident. Do you increase risk impulsively, or do you stick to your allocation?

Situation three. Nothing dramatic is happening. Your portfolio feels boring. Do you trade for excitement, or do you trust steady progress?

Each situation mirrors a softball moment.

Do you press when momentum shifts, or do you stay within yourself and execute fundamentals?

Common Athlete Mistakes and Financial Parallels

Athletes sometimes abandon mechanics under pressure. Investors abandon plans during volatility.

Athletes sometimes chase highlights to change momentum. Investors chase hot trends to feel productive.

Athletes sometimes confuse confidence with recklessness. Investors take unnecessary risks when things are going well.

Awareness helps. Systems prevent repetition.

Execution is not about intensity. It is about consistency.

Winning the Long Game

Buying and holding is not about being stubborn.

It is about being disciplined.

You cannot control markets. You cannot control headlines. You cannot control short-term outcomes. You can control behavior.

The investors who succeed are not smarter. They are steadier. They stay in the game. They trust the plan. They adjust when life truly changes, not when emotions spike.

Execution matters.

Trust the work. Trust the plan. Stay composed.

That is how championships are won, and that is how wealth is built over time.

Athlete Takeaways

- Open the right accounts and fund them consistently
- Execution matters more than perfect timing
- Buy-and-hold rewards discipline, not emotion
- Systems beat willpower under pressure
- Trust the plan and play the next pitch

Chapter 17: Rebalancing and Mid-Game Adjustments

Good teams do not wait until the final inning to make adjustments. They check in between innings. They talk through what is working and what is not. They tweak positioning, sequencing, and approach without scrapping the entire game plan. Nobody panics. Nobody reinvents the sport. The goal is to stay aligned with reality as the game unfolds.

Rebalancing serves that same purpose in investing.

It is not about reacting to noise or predicting what happens next. It is about maintaining balance as conditions change so risk stays aligned with your goals.

How Often to Review Investments

Reviewing is not the same as changing.

This distinction matters more than most people realize. Many investors review too often and adjust too much. Others avoid reviewing altogether and hope for the best. Neither approach works well.

A reasonable review schedule is usually quarterly or annually.

That cadence gives you enough information to stay aware without letting emotion hijack decisions. You can spot drift, confirm alignment, and note changes without reacting to every market move.

Athletes understand this rhythm naturally.

You review film after games, not during every pitch. You look for trends, not single mistakes. One bad at bat does not require a new swing. One great at bat does not mean everything is perfect.

Reviews should answer simple questions.

Is my allocation still aligned with my goals and time horizon?

Have certain positions grown or shrunk meaningfully?

Has my income, lifestyle, or responsibility changed?

If the answers raise concerns, adjustment may be appropriate. If not, staying put is often the smartest move. Action is not required simply because information exists.

Rebalancing Strategies

Rebalancing means bringing your portfolio back to its intended allocation.

Over time, investments grow at different rates. Stocks may outperform bonds. One sector may surge. Another may lag. Without rebalancing, portfolios drift.

Drift is not inherently bad.

In fact, drift is expected. But unmanaged drift quietly changes risk. A portfolio that started balanced can become aggressive without you realizing it. Or it can become overly conservative after periods of stress.

Rebalancing corrects that.

There are several common approaches.

Time-based rebalancing happens on a schedule, such as once per year. You rebalance regardless of market conditions.

Threshold-based rebalancing happens when allocations move beyond predefined ranges. For example, if stocks drift five percent above target, you rebalance.

Contribution-based rebalancing uses new money to restore balance. Instead of selling what has grown, you add to what has lagged.

The method matters less than consistency.

Rebalancing enforces discipline. It nudges you to trim what has run ahead and add to what has fallen behind. That feels uncomfortable emotionally because it goes against instinct. But strategically, it keeps risk aligned.

Athletes recognize this immediately.

If one part of the team starts doing too much while another falls behind, performance suffers. You restore balance so the system functions properly.

Life Changes and Portfolio Updates

Some adjustments are driven by markets.

Others are driven by life.

Life-driven changes matter more.

Job changes. Income shifts. Marriage. Children. Relocation. Health events. Approaching major goals. These developments alter risk capacity far more than market headlines ever will.

A portfolio built for one season of life may not fit the next.

An athlete early in their career plays differently than one nearing the end. Roles change. Minutes shift. Strategy evolves. Ignoring those changes leads to misalignment.

Updating your portfolio when life changes is not market timing.

It is situational awareness.

Ignoring life changes keeps you stuck in a strategy that no longer fits. Overreacting to them creates instability. The goal is thoughtful adjustment, not constant overhaul.

Avoiding Over-Adjustment

Over-adjustment is one of the most common investing mistakes.

Every headline feels urgent. Every market move feels meaningful. Constant tinkering feels productive. In reality, it often produces worse outcomes.

Athletes know this pattern well.

Changing mechanics mid-game usually backfires. Confidence erodes. Timing disappears. Execution suffers. The team becomes reactive instead of composed.

The same thing happens financially.

If you find yourself wanting to change something every time markets move, the issue is not the portfolio. It is the process.

Clear rules help here.

Scheduled reviews. Rebalancing thresholds. Written plans created during calm periods. These act as guardrails when emotion shows up.

Doing less, more intentionally, usually works better.

The Investing Concept Explained Through the Sport

Rebalancing is a between-innings adjustment.

You do not scrap the game plan. You fine-tune.

Life changes are lineup changes. Roles shift. Strategy adapts.

Over-adjustment is panic. Discipline is staying aligned with the system.

Winning teams do not confuse movement with progress. They adjust with purpose.

Coach's Perspective: What Would Your Coach Say?

A coach would keep it grounded.

"Make the adjustment, not the excuse."

"Stick to fundamentals."

"Do not overreact."

"Trust the system."

Financially, that means reviewing with intention, rebalancing when necessary, and avoiding constant change driven by emotion. Coaches do not want chaos in the dugout. Investors should not want it in their portfolios either.

Game Situations and Decision Points

Situation one. Stocks have outperformed and now dominate your portfolio. Risk is higher than planned. Do you rebalance or let drift continue unchecked?

Situation two. Markets struggle and bonds feel safer. Do you abandon growth entirely or restore balance intentionally?

Situation three. Your life changes significantly. New job. New family responsibilities. New timeline. Do you update your strategy or ignore reality?

Each situation mirrors a mid-game decision.

Do you stay composed and execute, or do you panic and overcorrect?

Common Athlete Mistakes and Financial Parallels

Athletes sometimes chase what just worked instead of trusting fundamentals. Investors chase recent winners.

Athletes sometimes overhaul everything after one mistake. Investors over-adjust after volatility.

Athletes sometimes ignore evolving roles. Investors ignore life transitions.

Awareness corrects these patterns. Systems reinforce better behavior.

Winning the Long Game

Rebalancing is not about perfection.

It is about discipline.

It keeps risk aligned with goals. It reduces emotional decision-making. It reinforces process over reaction. It prevents small drifts from turning into big problems.

Smart teams adjust without panicking.

Smart investors do the same.

Stay aware. Stay balanced. Stay composed.

That is how seasons are managed, and that is how long-term success is built.

Athlete Takeaways

- Review regularly, not constantly
- Rebalance to restore discipline, not chase performance
- Let life changes drive strategy updates
- Avoid over-adjustment under pressure
- Trust the system and make measured moves

Chapter 18: The Mental Side of Money

Softball teaches you quickly that the game is not just physical.

You can have the skills. You can have the preparation. You can put in the reps when nobody is watching. But when pressure rises, when the game tightens, and when the noise gets loud, the mental side decides outcomes. Confidence shifts. Momentum swings. One mistake can either stay isolated or snowball into something bigger. The teams that stay composed execute. The ones that spiral beat themselves.

Money is no different.

Most financial mistakes are not caused by lack of knowledge. They are caused by emotion. Pressure, comparison, fear, impatience, and overconfidence quietly hijack good plans. This chapter is about mastering the mental side of money so discipline holds when it matters most.

Pressure, Confidence, and Momentum

Pressure shows up when outcomes feel important.

A large purchase. A market drop. A job change. A sudden bonus or windfall. In these moments, decisions feel heavier. The stakes feel higher. Pressure can sharpen focus, or it can cause rushed mistakes.

Athletes know this feeling well.

Tight games magnify everything. A routine ground ball suddenly feels harder. Confidence becomes fragile. Momentum feels real, even when nothing fundamental has changed. One misstep can shake belief if it is not handled correctly.

Financial confidence works the same way.

When things are going well, plans feel easy to follow. Markets are calm. Income is steady. Confidence is high. When setbacks appear, doubt creeps in. People abandon plans not because the plan stopped working, but because confidence cracked under pressure.

Momentum in money is often psychological.

One good habit leads to another. Automatic saving builds investing confidence. Staying disciplined through one downturn makes the next easier. The opposite is also true. One emotional decision can lead to another if not checked.

Managing momentum means responding intentionally instead of emotionally. Pressure does not have to change your approach unless you let it.

Crowd Noise and Comparison

Crowd noise affects everyone.

In softball, crowds cheer, boo, and react to every play. None of that changes what you need to do next, but it is easy to let it seep in. Financially, comparison creates the same distraction.

Social media, coworkers, teammates, and family all create noise. Who bought a house. Who made a big investment. Who seems ahead. Who looks like they figured it out faster. Comparison turns money into a scoreboard it was never meant to be.

Athletes already understand this lesson.

Playing someone else's game leads to mistakes. Trying to copy another player's style instead of trusting your own training usually backfires. Everyone has different roles, strengths, and responsibilities.

Financial plans are personal.

Different incomes. Different timelines. Different family situations. Different risk tolerance. Comparing outcomes without context creates pressure that leads to bad decisions. People stretch too far. Take risks that do not fit. Abandon plans that were working.

The goal is progress, not comparison.

If your plan is moving you forward, noise does not matter. Crowd reaction is not strategy.

Building Systems for Discipline

Discipline does not come from motivation.

It comes from systems.

Athletes rely on structure. Practice schedules. Weight programs. Film sessions. Recovery routines. These systems remove decision-making from moments of fatigue or stress. You do not decide whether to train every day. The schedule decides for you.

Money needs the same support.

Automatic savings. Automatic investing. Scheduled reviews. Clear rules around spending and risk. These systems act like coaches when emotions spike. They keep you aligned with your plan even when confidence wavers.

Without systems, discipline depends on willpower.

Willpower fades under pressure. It disappears when life gets busy. Systems endure.

This is not about removing choice. It is about protecting good decisions from bad moments. Systems create consistency when emotion would otherwise interfere.

Staying Composed After Mistakes

Mistakes are inevitable.

Bad investments. Overspending. Missed opportunities. Delayed action. Everyone has them. Long-term success is not determined by avoiding mistakes. It is determined by how mistakes are handled.

Athletes are trained for this.

You make an error. You reset. You take a breath. You focus on the next play. You do not carry the mistake into the next pitch. Coaches preach this relentlessly because they know spirals lose games.

Financially, many people do the opposite.

They panic. They overcorrect. They try to make up for mistakes with bigger risks. They chase losses. They abandon structure. That turns one mistake into many.

Composure matters more than perfection.

Acknowledging a mistake, learning from it, and returning to the plan preserves momentum. Beating yourself up does not improve outcomes. Neither does pretending mistakes did not happen.

Resetting quickly is a skill. It can be practiced.

The Investing Concept Explained Through the Sport

The mental side of money is game management.

Pressure tests confidence. Crowd noise creates distraction. Systems replace emotion. Composure prevents spirals.

Just like in softball, the goal is not to avoid mistakes entirely. That is unrealistic. The goal is to respond correctly when they happen.

Championship teams are not error-free. They are resilient.

Coach's Perspective: What Would Your Coach Say?

A coach would not sugarcoat this.

"Control what you can control."

"Next play."

"Stay composed."

"Trust your training."

Financially, that means sticking to systems, ignoring noise, and responding calmly to setbacks. Coaches do not want players replaying mistakes in their heads. Investors should not either.

You cannot control markets. You can control behavior.

Game Situations and Decision Points

Situation one. Markets drop and everyone is talking about it. Headlines are loud. Group chats are buzzing. Do you react emotionally or stick to your system?

Situation two. Someone close to you makes a flashy financial move and talks about it constantly. Do you compare and chase, or stay focused on your own plan?

Situation three. You make a financial mistake. A poor purchase. A missed opportunity. Do you spiral and try to fix it immediately, or reset and return to fundamentals?

Each situation mirrors a mental test athletes face regularly. The skill is not eliminating pressure. It is managing it.

Common Athlete Mistakes and Financial Parallels

Athletes sometimes let one mistake turn into many. Investors chase losses after a bad decision.

Athletes sometimes play to the crowd instead of the situation. Investors chase trends instead of plans.

Athletes sometimes rely on emotion instead of structure. Investors abandon systems when things feel uncomfortable.

Mental discipline fixes these patterns. Structure reinforces it.

Winning the Long Game

Money rewards composure.

Not constant confidence. Not perfect decisions. Composure.

The athletes who succeed long term are not the ones who never struggle. They are the ones who respond well to struggle. They reset faster. They trust preparation. They stay disciplined when things get uncomfortable.

Build systems. Ignore noise. Reset quickly. Trust the process.

That is how momentum is protected on the field, and that is how long-term financial success is built.

Athlete Takeaways

- Pressure tests confidence, not preparation
- Comparison creates noise, not clarity
- Systems protect discipline under stress
- Mistakes are inevitable, spirals are optional
- Stay composed and play the next pitch

Part V: The Full Season and Life Beyond the Field

Every athlete eventually learns that the season does not last forever. Games end. Roles change. Schedules open up. The structure that once dictated your days fades, and a new kind of responsibility takes its place. What you built during the season matters, but how you carry it forward matters more.

Money follows the same arc.

This section of the book looks beyond the mechanics of investing and focuses on how financial decisions intersect with real life. Taxes. Housing. Careers. Family. Legacy. These are not separate topics. They are part of one long season made up of many chapters.

Early in life, the focus is often survival and growth. Later, it shifts to balance and protection. Eventually, it becomes about purpose, stewardship, and impact. Smart athletes adapt to these shifts without clinging to old roles that no longer fit.

This section emphasizes context.

A financial decision that makes sense at one stage can be a mistake at another. Renting may be right before buying. Aggressive saving may matter more than aggressive investing. Career choices may outweigh portfolio returns. The scoreboard changes, and strategy must change with it.

You will also see how money decisions ripple outward. Housing affects flexibility. Career decisions affect income and benefits. Family conversations affect expectations and boundaries. Estate planning affects people you may never meet. These choices extend far beyond accounts and balances.

Athletes understand seasons. Offseasons matter as much as game days. Preparation never really stops, but focus shifts. Financial life works the same way.

This part of the book helps you zoom out and think long term without losing clarity in the present. It is about playing the full season well, not just winning early innings.

Life beyond the field does not come with a coach, a practice schedule, or a playbook. This section helps you build one.

The goal is not to replace sports. It is to carry forward the discipline, awareness, and adaptability sports taught you into the next phase of life.

Finish strong. Stay intentional. Respect the long season.

That is how athletes win beyond the field.

Chapter 19: Taxes and Where You Place the Ball

In softball, where you place the ball matters.

You can square one up perfectly and hit it right at a defender for an out. You can take a slightly different swing, find a gap, and suddenly the inning changes. The mechanics may look the same from the stands, but placement changes results.

Taxes work the same way.

It is not just how much you earn or how much you invest. It is where those dollars are placed. Two athletes can earn the same amount and invest the same way, yet end up with very different outcomes simply because one understood placement and the other ignored it.

Understanding taxes does not require becoming an expert. It requires knowing the rules well enough to stop giving away runs.

Taxable vs Tax-Advantaged Accounts

Taxable accounts are straightforward.

You invest money that has already been taxed. As the account grows, you pay taxes on interest, dividends, and realized gains when you sell. There are no special restrictions on when you can access the money. Flexibility is the benefit.

Tax-advantaged accounts exist to encourage long-term saving.

These accounts provide tax benefits either now or later. The benefit is efficiency, not flexibility. Rules exist around contributions, withdrawals, and timing because the government is rewarding long-term behavior.

The key difference between these accounts is timing.

Taxable accounts give you freedom. Tax-advantaged accounts give you leverage.

Most people need both.

Athletes understand this instinctively. Sometimes you need flexibility to react to the game. Other times you need structure to stay disciplined. Using the right tool in the right situation improves outcomes without requiring extra effort.

The mistake is using only one type of account for everything. That limits options and creates unnecessary tax drag.

Tax-Deferred vs Tax-Free Growth

Tax-advantaged accounts generally fall into two categories: tax-deferred and tax-free.

Tax-deferred accounts allow your investments to grow without paying taxes each year. Taxes are paid later, when money is withdrawn. This can be powerful because compounding happens on a larger base when taxes are delayed.

Tax-free accounts work differently.

Money goes in after taxes, but growth and qualified withdrawals come out tax-free. There is no bill later if rules are followed. That certainty has value.

Both have roles.

Tax-deferred growth is often useful when you expect to be in a lower tax bracket later than you are today. Tax-free growth is powerful when you expect higher taxes in the future or simply want certainty and flexibility.

This is not about predicting the future perfectly.

It is about balancing risk.

Athletes make similar decisions constantly. You play aggressively early when there is time to recover. You protect late when the margin is thin. Timing changes strategy. Taxes work the same way.

Asset Location Basics

Asset location is about placing investments in the most tax-efficient accounts.

This is different from asset allocation. Allocation is what you own. Location is where you hold it.

Some investments generate income that is taxed every year. Others grow primarily through price appreciation and can be held longer before taxes are triggered. Placing these investments intentionally reduces tax drag over time.

This does not require complexity.

It requires awareness.

Placing tax-inefficient investments in tax-advantaged accounts keeps more of the return working for you. Placing more tax-efficient investments in taxable accounts preserves flexibility while minimizing annual tax impact.

Athletes do this instinctively on the field.

You do not put slow players in positions that require range. You do not put your strongest arm where it will not be used. You match roles to strengths.

Asset location follows the same logic. Same players. Better positioning.

Common Tax Mistakes

Many tax mistakes are unforced errors.

Ignoring taxes entirely until a bill shows up. Selling investments without understanding the consequences. Using the wrong account for a specific goal. Withdrawing early and triggering penalties. Assuming a large refund means success.

Refunds are not trophies.

They often mean you gave the government an interest-free loan. That may be unavoidable sometimes, but it should not be mistaken for winning.

Another common mistake is letting taxes dominate every decision.

Avoiding taxes at all costs often leads to worse outcomes. People hold bad investments too long. They skip opportunities that would still make sense after tax. They contort plans around fear instead of efficiency.

Taxes should inform decisions, not control them.

Athletes know this balance. You respect the rules, but you do not play scared. Smart play beats hesitation.

The Investing Concept Explained Through the Sport

Taxes are defensive positioning.

They do not change how hard you swing. They change where the ball lands. Smart positioning turns the same effort into better outcomes. Poor positioning wastes solid contact.

You do not need exotic strategies to improve tax outcomes. You need awareness, planning, and intentional placement.

Coach's Perspective: What Would Your Coach Say?

A coach would be direct.

"Know the rules."

"Play smart."

"Do not give away outs."

Financially, that means understanding basic tax mechanics and placing assets intentionally. Coaches lose their minds over mental errors. Tax mistakes fall into that category.

Game Situations and Decision Points

Situation one. You want to invest for the long term. Do you use a taxable account because it feels simple, or a tax-advantaged account because efficiency matters?

Situation two. You sell an investment for a gain. Do you plan for taxes ahead of time, or are you surprised later?

Situation three. You save consistently for retirement but choose the wrong account type. Does that reduce flexibility when you actually need the money?

Each situation mirrors a placement decision on the field. The swing may be the same. The outcome depends on where the ball goes.

Common Athlete Mistakes and Financial Parallels

Athletes sometimes swing hard without regard for placement. Investors focus on returns and ignore taxes.

Athletes sometimes forget situational rules. Investors forget tax rules until it is too late.

Athletes sometimes give away outs. Investors give away dollars.

Awareness fixes these mistakes. Preparation prevents them.

Winning the Long Game

Taxes will always exist.

Ignoring them does not make them go away. Overreacting to them creates fear-based decisions. The sweet spot is understanding.

Knowing where to place the ball keeps more runs on the board. Over time, that difference compounds quietly but powerfully.

You do not need perfection.

You need intention.

Understand the rules. Match the tool to the situation. Place the ball wisely and let the season work in your favor.

Athlete Takeaways

- Placement matters as much as effort
- Taxable accounts provide flexibility, tax-advantaged accounts provide efficiency
- Tax-deferred and tax-free growth both have roles
- Asset location reduces unnecessary drag
- Know the rules so you stop giving away runs

Chapter 20: Retirement Accounts and Financial Independence

Retirement feels far away to most athletes.

When your focus has always been the next season, the next rep, the next opportunity, thinking decades ahead feels abstract. Life has trained you to live in short windows. Prepare for the game. Compete. Recover. Repeat. Long timelines feel theoretical.

But athletes also understand something most people do not.

Careers are finite. Bodies change. Windows close faster than expected. Opportunities that feel permanent rarely are. Planning ahead is not pessimism. It is professionalism.

Retirement accounts exist to turn today's effort into future freedom.

They are not about quitting life or sitting still. They are about creating options when your priorities shift. They are about reducing pressure later by doing disciplined work now.

Employer Plans and Pensions

Many athletes first encounter retirement saving through an employer plan.

These plans allow you to contribute automatically from your paycheck. Money goes in before you ever see it. That matters more than people realize. When saving happens automatically, discipline replaces decision-making.

Some employers offer matching contributions.

That match is extra compensation. It is money added to your account simply because you showed up and participated. Ignoring it is like leaving money on the bench during a close game. You already earned it. You just have to claim it.

Pensions are less common today, but when they exist, they provide guaranteed income later in life. Understanding how pensions vest, how benefits are calculated, and what happens if you leave early matters. These plans reward longevity and consistency.

Athletes understand this model instinctively.

Show up. Put in reps. Earn benefits over time.

Employer plans work best when you treat them like training programs. You do not negotiate with your alarm clock every morning. You follow the schedule. Contributions should feel the same way.

Traditional and Roth IRAs

Individual retirement accounts provide additional flexibility beyond employer plans.

Traditional IRAs offer tax-deferred growth. Contributions may reduce taxable income now. Investments grow without annual tax drag. Taxes are paid later when money is withdrawn.

Roth IRAs flip that structure.

Contributions are made with after-tax dollars. Growth happens tax free. Qualified withdrawals come out tax free. There is no future tax bill if rules are followed.

Neither option is universally better.

The right choice depends on your current income, expected future taxes, and flexibility needs. Someone early in their career may benefit from different strategies than someone at peak earnings. Certainty can be just as valuable as deferral.

Athletes understand this from training cycles.

Sometimes you push hard now to build a base. Sometimes you protect energy for later. Strategy changes based on context, not emotion.

Using both types of accounts over time can create balance. Flexibility matters in long careers.

Contribution and Withdrawal Rules

Retirement accounts come with rules.

Contribution limits cap how much you can add each year. These limits change over time and differ by account type. Exceeding them creates penalties.

Withdrawal rules matter just as much.

Money in retirement accounts is designed for later stages of life. Withdrawing too early often triggers taxes and penalties. These penalties are not there to punish you. They are there to protect the long-term purpose of the account.

Ignoring these rules leads to unforced errors.

Athletes know how damaging eligibility mistakes can be. Using an ineligible player can cost games, seasons, or championships. Breaking retirement account rules costs money and future opportunity.

Knowing the rules keeps you from beating yourself.

Retirement Income Basics

Retirement is not an age.

It is a phase.

Income in retirement usually comes from multiple sources. Employer plans. Individual accounts. Personal savings. Social benefits. Sometimes ongoing work or business income.

The goal is not necessarily to stop working.

The goal is financial independence.

Having choices. Reducing pressure. Deciding how and when you work based on preference instead of necessity.

Athletes understand this desire deeply.

You want control over your schedule. You want to protect your body and energy. You want to compete on your terms. Financial independence creates that same freedom off the field.

Planning income streams ahead of time reduces stress later. It allows you to adjust gradually instead of reacting under pressure. Flexibility matters as much as totals.

The Investing Concept Explained Through the Sport

Retirement accounts are long seasons.

You train early. You build steadily. You protect progress. Eventually, you rely on what you built.

Skipping early reps does not make success impossible, but it makes it harder. Consistency compounds. Time matters.

Athletes who succeed long term understand this. Development is rarely linear. Quiet years matter just as much as breakout moments.

Money works the same way.

Coach's Perspective: What Would Your Coach Say?

A coach would not complicate this.

"Start early."

"Use the system."

"Do not waste reps."

"Play the long game."

Financially, that means contributing consistently, understanding the rules, and letting time work for you. Coaches do not wait until playoffs to start conditioning. Investors should not wait until later years to start saving.

Game Situations and Decision Points

Situation one. Your employer offers a match. Do you contribute enough to receive it, or do you tell yourself you will start later?

Situation two. You receive extra income. Do you invest it for long-term independence or let it disappear into lifestyle upgrades?

Situation three. You consider withdrawing early from a retirement account. Do you understand the penalties and long-term impact?

Each situation mirrors long-term development choices athletes face. Short-term comfort versus long-term opportunity.

Common Athlete Mistakes and Financial Parallels

Athletes sometimes assume they have more time. Investors delay retirement saving.

Athletes sometimes skip conditioning when results feel far away. Investors skip contributions because benefits feel distant.

Athletes sometimes break rules under pressure. Investors make early withdrawals without understanding consequences.

Awareness prevents these mistakes. Structure reinforces discipline.

Winning the Long Game

Retirement accounts are not about age.

They are about freedom.

They are about turning discipline into options. Effort into flexibility. Time into independence.

Consistent contributions matter more than perfect strategy. Understanding rules prevents unnecessary losses. Patience allows compounding to work quietly in the background.

Financial independence is not built in one moment. It is built the same way championships are built.

Day by day. Rep by rep. Season by season.

Train now. Benefit later.

Athlete Takeaways

- Employer matches are extra compensation you already earned
- Traditional and Roth accounts serve different roles
- Rules matter and penalties are avoidable
- Retirement is about choice, not stopping
- Start early, stay consistent, and play the long game

Chapter 21: Housing and Major Financial Decisions

Some decisions change the feel of the entire season.

A position change. A new role in the lineup. A coaching change. These moments do not just affect one game. They reshape routines, confidence, and long-term development. Housing and other major financial decisions work the same way. They shape cash flow, flexibility, and stress levels for years, sometimes decades.

This chapter is about slowing those decisions down and making them intentionally instead of emotionally.

Renting vs Buying

Renting and buying are not opposing teams. They are different tools.

Renting buys flexibility. It allows you to move cities, change jobs, adjust lifestyles, and adapt to uncertainty without being locked into a long-term commitment. For athletes early in careers, or anyone whose income, location, or priorities are still shifting, renting often makes sense.

Buying creates stability and the potential to build equity over time. It can anchor you to a location, create predictable housing costs, and support long-term planning. For athletes and professionals with stable income and a clear sense of where life is headed, ownership can fit well.

The mistake is treating buying as a milestone instead of a strategy.

Athletes understand timing. You do not force a promotion before you are ready. You do not change positions without understanding the tradeoffs. Buying a home too early can limit flexibility and increase pressure. Renting too long once stability exists can delay equity building.

The right choice depends on time horizon, income reliability, location, and personal goals. There is no universal rule, only situational awareness.

Mortgages and Down Payments

A mortgage is leverage.

It allows you to control a large asset with a smaller upfront investment. Leverage magnifies outcomes. It can help build wealth when things go well. It can amplify stress when income becomes uncertain.

Down payments affect everything.

Larger down payments lower monthly payments, reduce interest costs, and provide more breathing room. Smaller down payments preserve cash but increase leverage and monthly obligations. Neither approach is automatically right or wrong.

Athletes understand leverage intuitively. Playing aggressive defense can shift momentum. It can also backfire if timing is wrong. The same play can look brilliant or reckless depending on context.

One of the biggest mistakes buyers make is confusing approval with affordability.

Just because a lender approves a certain amount does not mean it fits your life. Approval reflects lending rules, not your comfort level. It does not account for stress, lifestyle goals, or how you want money to feel month to month.

Comfort matters. Sleep matters. Financial pressure affects performance in every other area of life. The best mortgage decision balances affordability, flexibility, and long-term comfort, not maximum borrowing.

Cars, Leases, and Financing Traps

Cars are one of the most common financial traps athletes fall into.

They are necessary. They are visible. They are emotional. They also lose value quickly.

Financing a depreciating asset over long periods creates drag on cash flow. Low monthly payments hide total cost. Leases feel affordable, but they often reset every few years, keeping people in a permanent payment cycle.

Athletes understand equipment choices. You want gear that performs reliably, not gear that drains energy and attention. The same logic applies here.

Cars should support your life, not define it.

Reliability matters more than image. Cash flow matters more than appearances. A vehicle that allows you to save, invest, and sleep well beats one that impresses strangers.

The trap is upgrading too early or too often. Lifestyle inflation shows up fast in transportation decisions, especially when income increases suddenly.

Planning Major Purchases

Major purchases deserve planning.

Homes, vehicles, relocations, and other large commitments shape your financial posture for years. These decisions should align with long-term goals, not short-term emotion.

Pressure often comes from comparison.

Friends buying homes. Teammates upgrading cars. Social media celebrating milestones. Noise creates urgency that has nothing to do with readiness.

Athletes know this feeling. Crowd noise does not change the game plan. Execution still matters.

Before making a major purchase, ask simple questions.

Does this decision increase or reduce flexibility?

How does it affect monthly cash flow?

What happens if income changes?

Does this support the life I want in five or ten years?

If answers create discomfort, that is information. Pausing is not failure. It is discipline.

The Investing Concept Explained Through the Sport

Housing and major purchases are positioning decisions.

They affect how much risk you can take elsewhere. High fixed expenses reduce flexibility. Lower fixed expenses increase options.

Smart teams think about field position before calling plays. Smart financial decisions consider positioning before committing.

Once committed, adjustments become harder. That is why planning matters more here than almost anywhere else.

Coach's Perspective: What Would Your Coach Say?

A coach would slow the moment down.

"Know the situation."

"Do not force it."

"Stay within yourself."

"Think long term."

Financially, that means not rushing big decisions to satisfy ego or pressure. Coaches do not want players freelancing in critical moments. Financial discipline matters most when stakes are high.

Game Situations and Decision Points

Situation one. You feel pressure to buy because everyone around you is doing it. Do you evaluate readiness or follow noise?

Situation two. You qualify for a much larger mortgage than expected. Do you borrow the maximum or choose comfort?

Situation three. Your income increases and a new car feels justified. Do you plan intentionally or react emotionally?

Each situation mirrors a softball decision. Do you rush the play, or do you let it develop?

Common Athlete Mistakes and Financial Parallels

Athletes sometimes rush into roles before mastering fundamentals. Buyers rush ownership before stability.

Athletes sometimes play for the crowd. Buyers chase appearances.

Athletes sometimes ignore fatigue. Buyers ignore cash flow strain.

Awareness prevents these mistakes. Discipline corrects them.

Winning the Long Game

Housing and major purchases are not about winning today.

They are about sustaining performance over years.

Flexibility is an advantage. Comfort is underrated. Discipline protects future choices.

The goal is not to maximize what you can buy. The goal is to build a life that supports consistency, confidence, and freedom.

Make decisions that support the season you want to play, not just the moment you are in.

Athlete Takeaways

- Renting buys flexibility, buying buys stability
- Approval does not equal affordability
- Leverage magnifies comfort or stress
- Cars should support life, not drain it
- Plan major purchases like game-changing plays

Chapter 22: Your Career Is Your Strongest Position

In softball, position matters.

Where you play determines how often the ball finds you, how much impact you have, and how long you stay on the field. Some positions touch the ball every play. Others influence the game quietly through leadership and consistency. No matter where you line up, your position shapes the entire season.

Your career works the same way.

Your career is the position you play every day. It drives income, benefits, flexibility, and opportunity. Investing matters, but your ability to earn, grow, and adapt matters more, especially early and mid-career. This chapter is about treating your career with the same intentionality you brought to your sport.

Salary vs Total Compensation

Many people focus only on salary. That is understandable. Salary is visible. It hits the bank account. It feels tangible.

But salary is only part of the picture.

Total compensation includes benefits like retirement matches, health insurance, bonuses, equity, paid time off, and flexibility. Two jobs with the same salary can have very different real value once benefits are considered.

Athletes understand this concept intuitively. Playing time is not the only measure of value. Role, trust, development, and longevity matter too.

A slightly lower salary with strong benefits and growth opportunities can outperform a higher salary with weak support and burnout risk. Evaluating total compensation leads to better long-term decisions.

Job Changes and Benefits

Changing teams changes everything.

New systems. New expectations. New culture. New benefits. Every job change deserves a full review, not just excitement about the offer.

Benefits matter more than most people realize. Health insurance quality affects risk. Retirement plans affect long-term growth. Disability coverage affects income protection. Time off affects recovery and performance.

Athletes study new programs before committing. They ask questions. They understand roles. Career moves deserve the same preparation.

Do not assume benefits are equal. Do not assume what worked before still applies. Each move changes the game plan.

Negotiation Basics

Negotiation does not mean confrontation.

It means communication.

Athletes negotiate roles all the time, often without calling it that. Conversations about playing time, expectations, and development are negotiations. Respectful. Direct. Informed.

Career negotiation works best the same way.

Know your value. Understand the role. Ask thoughtful questions. Focus on fit, not just numbers. Silence is not weakness. Preparation is strength.

Negotiation is not about winning at the other side's expense. It is about alignment. When both sides understand expectations, outcomes improve.

Avoiding negotiation entirely is like never speaking up in a team meeting. It limits growth.

Side Income and Entrepreneurship

Side income is becoming more common, especially for athletes who value autonomy.

Coaching. Consulting. Content creation. Small businesses. These opportunities can diversify income and build skills. They can also create distraction and burnout if unmanaged.

Athletes understand balance. Extra training can help or hurt depending on timing and recovery.

Side income should support your primary position, not undermine it. Time, taxes, and energy all matter. Starting small, testing ideas, and building gradually reduces risk.

Entrepreneurship is not for everyone. It requires discipline, patience, and tolerance for uncertainty. There is no shame in choosing stability. The goal is alignment, not image.

The Investing Concept Explained Through the Sport

Your career is your primary offensive position.

Investments support it. Savings protect it. Insurance defends it. But income drives everything else.

You can play great defense and still lose without offense. You can invest well, but without income growth, progress is limited.

Treat your career like your strongest position. Develop it. Protect it. Use it intentionally.

Coach's Perspective: What Would Your Coach Say?

"Do your job."

"Know your role."

"Communicate."

"Get better every day."

Financially, that means understanding your compensation, advocating for yourself appropriately, and continuing to develop skills. Coaches expect players to take ownership of their roles. Careers demand the same.

Game Situations and Decision Points

Situation one. You receive a job offer with higher salary but weaker benefits. Do you evaluate total compensation or focus on the headline number?

Situation two. You feel undervalued. Do you prepare and negotiate or quietly disengage?

Situation three. You consider a side project. Do you plan intentionally or jump in impulsively?

Each situation mirrors a position decision. Long-term impact matters.

Common Athlete Mistakes and Financial Parallels

Athletes sometimes chase stats instead of development. Professionals chase salary instead of growth.

Athletes sometimes ignore fit. Professionals ignore culture.

Athletes sometimes overtrain. Professionals overcommit.

Awareness prevents these mistakes.

Winning the Long Game

Your career will change roles over time.

Early years focus on development and reps. Mid-career emphasizes leverage and balance. Later years prioritize flexibility and purpose.

Strong careers are built intentionally, not accidentally. They reward those who understand their position and play it well.

Investing matters. But your career is the engine that powers everything else.

Athlete Takeaways

- Salary is only part of compensation
- Benefits affect long-term outcomes
- Preparation makes negotiation easier
- Side income should support, not distract
- Treat your career like your strongest position

Chapter 23: Estate Planning Basics Everyone Needs

Estate planning sounds like something reserved for later in life. Many athletes assume it is only for the wealthy, the retired, or the elderly. That assumption creates gaps that show up at the worst possible time. Estate planning is not about predicting the end. It is about preparation, protection, and clarity when things do not go as planned.

Athletes understand this mindset better than most.

You do not prepare for adversity because you expect disaster. You prepare so the team is not scrambling when something unexpected happens. Estate planning serves the same purpose. It keeps people protected, roles clear, and decisions aligned with your wishes when pressure is highest.

This chapter is about responsibility, not fear.

Wills and Trusts

A will is a set of instructions.

It outlines who receives your assets, who is responsible for carrying out those instructions, and who would care for dependents if something happens to you. Without a will, state law decides these outcomes. Those default rules may not reflect your relationships, values, or intentions.

A will does not move assets by itself. It provides direction. It creates clarity when clarity matters most.

A trust is a more flexible tool.

Trusts can control how and when assets are distributed, protect privacy, reduce complications, and help manage situations where beneficiaries are young, inexperienced, or vulnerable. Trusts are not just for large estates. They are for people who want control, organization, and smoother execution.

Athletes understand this difference intuitively.

A general game plan outlines intent. Position-specific assignments handle nuance. Wills set direction. Trusts manage execution.

The goal is not complexity. The goal is clarity.

Beneficiaries and Account Titling

One of the most misunderstood parts of estate planning is how assets actually transfer.

Many assets pass outside of a will.

Retirement accounts, life insurance policies, and certain investment accounts transfer based on beneficiary designations. Those designations override instructions in a will. If they are outdated or missing, outcomes can directly contradict your intentions.

This is where many well-meaning plans break down.

A former spouse still listed. A parent listed when circumstances have changed. No contingent beneficiaries named. These are not dramatic mistakes. They are administrative oversights that carry serious consequences.

Account titling also matters.

Individual ownership, joint ownership, and trust ownership all carry different implications for control, access, and transfer. Titling determines who can act, who inherits, and how smoothly assets move.

Athletes know how dangerous miscommunication can be.

One missed assignment changes everything. Estate planning works the same way. Details are not optional. They are the system.

Reviewing beneficiaries regularly is one of the simplest and most powerful steps you can take. Life changes faster than paperwork. Marriage, children, career changes, and relocations should all trigger reviews.

Powers of Attorney

A power of attorney authorizes someone to make financial decisions on your behalf if you cannot.

This document matters while you are alive, not after you are gone.

Without it, loved ones may be forced into court processes just to manage basic matters. Paying bills. Accessing accounts. Signing documents. These delays create stress during moments when focus should be elsewhere.

Power of attorney is about continuity.

Athletes never assume one player will be available forever. Depth matters. Backups matter. Power of attorney is financial depth. It ensures someone you trust can step in temporarily if needed.

Choosing the right person matters.

This role requires responsibility, judgment, and calm under pressure. It is not about favoritism. It is about fit. Athletes understand this distinction better than most.

Healthcare Directives

Healthcare directives communicate your medical wishes.

They outline what types of care you want or do not want and appoint someone to make decisions if you cannot speak for yourself. This is not about being dramatic. It is about reducing uncertainty for the people who care about you most.

In stressful medical situations, loved ones should not be guessing.

Athletes understand communication under pressure.

Clear signals prevent mistakes. Confusion creates hesitation. Healthcare directives provide clarity when emotions are high and time matters.

This is not just about outcomes. It is about dignity, values, and respect.

The Investing Concept Explained Through the Sport

Estate planning is game management off the field.

It does not affect daily performance. It does not show up on a scoreboard. But it protects the entire program when something unexpected happens.

It ensures continuity.

It assigns roles.

It reduces chaos.

It protects teammates and family.

Strong teams prepare beyond the obvious. Responsible individuals do the same.

Coach's Perspective: What Would Your Coach Say?

A coach would not overcomplicate this.

"Handle your business."

"Be prepared."

"Protect your team."

"Do not leave things unfinished."

Financially, that means having basic estate documents in place and keeping them updated. Coaches do not want leadership gaps when pressure hits. Life does not either.

Game Situations and Decision Points

Situation one. You have assets but no will. If something happens, does state law reflect your wishes?

Situation two. Your beneficiaries were set years ago. Do they still match your current life?

Situation three. You are temporarily incapacitated. Who can step in and handle financial or medical decisions?

Each situation mirrors a leadership gap. When roles are unclear, confusion follows. Preparation prevents that.

Common Athlete Mistakes and Financial Parallels

Athletes sometimes assume nothing will happen. People skip estate planning.

Athletes sometimes rely on verbal communication instead of written plans. People rely on unwritten wishes.

Athletes sometimes forget to update roles as teams change. People forget to update documents as life evolves.

These mistakes are common. They are also preventable.

Winning the Long Game

Estate planning is not about wealth.

It is about responsibility.

It protects people you care about. It reduces conflict. It preserves dignity, privacy, and intention. It allows loved ones to focus on healing instead of logistics.

You do not need perfection.

You need a plan.

Set up the basics. Review them periodically. Adjust when life changes. Handle the details now so others do not have to guess later.

That is leadership.

Athlete Takeaways

- Estate planning is preparation, not prediction
- Wills and trusts create clarity and control
- Beneficiary designations override assumptions
- Powers of attorney ensure continuity
- Clear directives protect your team

Chapter 24: Talking About Money With Family

Money changes when it involves other people.

What once felt like a personal decision becomes shared. Emotions rise. Assumptions appear. Old roles resurface. For many athletes, these conversations are harder than any game they played, not because they lack courage, but because money mixes identity, responsibility, history, and expectations.

This chapter is about approaching those conversations with clarity and leadership instead of avoidance or emotion.

Teaching Kids About Money

Athletes know fundamentals are learned early.

You do not wait until high school to teach throwing mechanics or footwork. You start young, repeat often, and focus on basics. Money works the same way. Kids learn from observation long before they understand numbers.

Teaching kids about money is less about lectures and more about habits.

How you spend. How you save. How you talk about money. How you handle mistakes. These behaviors shape beliefs long before formal lessons ever do.

Involving kids in simple decisions builds awareness. Giving them small responsibilities. Letting them save toward goals. Allowing age-appropriate mistakes. Shielding kids from everything delays development.

Overcontrolling creates confusion later.

Athletes understand this process instinctively.

You let younger players grow into responsibility. You coach them through mistakes. You expect effort and learning, not perfection. Financial education at home should feel the same way.

College and Young Adults

College and early adulthood are financial transition years.

Income changes. Expenses rise. Independence increases. Mistakes are common. This is not failure. It is development.

Parents and mentors often struggle here because the urge to protect competes with the need to teach. Doing everything for young adults prevents growth. Doing nothing leaves them unprepared.

Clear expectations matter.

Who pays for what. How budgets work. What support looks like. What happens if money runs out. What consequences exist. These conversations reduce confusion and resentment on both sides.

Athletes understand this balance.

Coaches support players while holding them accountable. They provide resources, structure, and guidance, but they do not remove responsibility. Families should do the same.

Support without structure creates dependence. Structure without support creates resentment. Balance creates growth.

Aging Parents and Caregiving

As life progresses, roles begin to reverse.

Money conversations with aging parents can be emotionally charged. Independence, pride, health, and fear are all intertwined. Parents may resist help. Children may feel unprepared or overwhelmed.

Waiting until a crisis makes everything harder.

Approaching these conversations early allows for planning instead of panic.

It creates space for respect instead of urgency. Topics may include budgeting, housing, insurance, healthcare decisions, and legal documents.

These conversations are not easy, but they are necessary.

Athletes know leadership is tested most in uncomfortable moments. Avoiding the conversation does not prevent the situation. It just delays preparation and increases stress later.

Leading here means listening, not dictating. It means offering support without taking control prematurely. It means focusing on dignity as much as logistics.

Family Expectations and Boundaries

Unspoken expectations cause conflict.

Who helps whom. How much support is expected. For how long. Under what conditions. What happens when resources are limited. These questions often go unanswered until tension erupts.

Boundaries are not about being selfish.

They are about clarity.

Athletes understand roles.

Clear roles prevent confusion. Clear boundaries protect team culture. When roles are unclear, resentment builds. Families function the same way.

Setting boundaries does not mean refusing to help. It means helping intentionally, with clear expectations and limits. Emotional reactions create inconsistency. Intentional decisions preserve relationships.

Boundaries allow generosity to exist without burnout.

The Investing Concept Explained Through the Sport

Talking about money with family is leadership.

It requires preparation, communication, and composure. You set tone. You define expectations. You manage pressure. You protect relationships.

Just like team leadership, avoidance creates problems. Clear communication builds trust and stability.

Coach's Perspective: What Would Your Coach Say?

A coach would not avoid this.

"Communicate."

"Be clear."

"Lead."

"Protect the locker room."

Financially, that means addressing money conversations directly and respectfully. Coaches do not allow confusion to fester. Families should not either.

Game Situations and Decision Points

Situation one. A child asks for financial help. Do you react emotionally, or do you explain expectations and limits?

Situation two. A young adult struggles financially. Do you step in completely, or do you guide development while allowing responsibility?

Situation three. A parent needs assistance. Do you wait for crisis, or do you plan ahead together?

Each situation mirrors leadership moments athletes face regularly. Calm leadership matters more than perfect answers.

Common Athlete Mistakes and Financial Parallels

Athletes sometimes avoid tough conversations. Families avoid money talks.

Athletes sometimes blur roles. Families blur boundaries.

Athletes sometimes lead with emotion under pressure. Families react instead of plan.

Awareness corrects these patterns. Preparation prevents them.

Winning the Long Game

Money conversations are not about control.

They are about clarity.

Handled well, they strengthen relationships. Handled poorly, they create resentment, confusion, and long-term strain. Leadership matters here as much as anywhere else in life.

Speak clearly. Set expectations. Stay composed. Revisit conversations as life changes.

That is how families win the long game together.

Athlete Takeaways

- Money conversations require leadership
- Teaching happens through habits, not lectures
- Clear expectations reduce conflict
- Boundaries protect relationships
- Preparation beats crisis

Part VI: Winning the Long Game

Every athlete eventually learns the difference between winning moments and winning careers.

Moments are loud. Wins are celebrated. Losses sting. Careers are quieter. They are built through decisions made when no one is watching, habits repeated when motivation fades, and discipline maintained long after the spotlight moves on.

Money works the same way.

This final section of the book focuses on longevity. Not just financial success, but financial stability, confidence, and resilience over decades. Winning the long game is not about maximizing every outcome. It is about avoiding mistakes that knock you out and reinforcing habits that keep you moving forward.

Athletes understand this concept deeply. You do not train for one game. You train to stay healthy, competitive, and relevant over time. You manage recovery. You listen to your body. You adapt as roles change. Financial life requires the same awareness.

This section brings everything together.

You will learn how to recognize when professional help makes sense and how to avoid scams and bad advice that target confidence and urgency. You will revisit common mistakes athletes and non-athletes alike make and learn how to sidestep them before damage compounds.

Most importantly, this section reinforces mindset.

Long-term success is not about being smarter than everyone else. It is about being steadier. It is about understanding that discipline beats intensity, process beats prediction, and consistency beats shortcuts.

There will always be noise. New products. New trends. New opinions. The long game requires filtering that noise and sticking to principles that do not change.

Athletes who succeed after sports are not the ones who chase every opportunity. They are the ones who evaluate fit, protect progress, and make decisions aligned with their values and goals.

This section is not about perfection. It is about sustainability.

If you commit to playing the long game with money the same way you committed to your sport, showing up, staying coachable, and respecting fundamentals, you will put yourself in position to win long after the final whistle or last out.

The season may change. The game plan may evolve. But the goal remains the same.

Stay in the game. Finish strong. Win the long game.

Chapter 25: Advisors, Scams, and Long-Term Success

Every athlete eventually reaches a point where talent and effort are not enough by themselves.

At higher levels, everyone works hard. Everyone is skilled. The difference comes from coaching, preparation, and decision-making. The same thing happens with money. As life becomes more complex, trying to do everything alone often creates blind spots.

This chapter is about knowing when to get help, how to choose it wisely, and how to protect yourself from people and ideas that promise shortcuts.

When to Seek Professional Help

Needing help is not weakness. It is awareness.

Athletes work with coaches, trainers, nutritionists, and medical staff because outside perspective matters. Money deserves the same respect.

Professional help often makes sense when:

- Your financial life becomes more complex
- Major life transitions occur
- You feel overwhelmed or uncertain
- Mistakes would be costly or hard to unwind

Taxes, investments, insurance, estate planning, business income, and family dynamics can intersect quickly. When decisions start affecting multiple areas at once, guidance adds value.

The goal is not to outsource responsibility. The goal is to add perspective and structure so decisions improve.

Types of Financial Advisors

Not all advisors play the same role.

Some focus on investments. Some focus on planning. Some focus on insurance. Some combine multiple areas. Understanding this prevents mismatched expectations.

Fee-based and fee-only advisors are compensated through fees rather than commissions, though structures vary. Commission-based advisors earn income through product sales. Neither model guarantees good advice. Alignment and transparency matter more.

A good advisor helps you clarify goals, build systems, and stay disciplined. A bad one sells complexity, creates dependency, or pressures urgency.

Athletes understand fit. A great pitching coach is not always a great hitting coach. Financial help works the same way.

Ask questions. Understand compensation. Know what services are provided. Trust is built through clarity, not credentials alone.

Recognizing Scams and Bad Advice

Scams target emotion.

Urgency. Exclusivity. Fear. Confidence without substance. These tactics work because they bypass logic.

Common red flags include:

- Guaranteed returns
- Pressure to act immediately
- Complex explanations that discourage questions
- Appeals to status or insider access

- Dismissal of risk

Bad advice is not always illegal. Sometimes it is simply misaligned. Advice that ignores your time horizon, risk tolerance, or goals is dangerous even if it sounds smart.

Athletes know the difference between confidence and recklessness. Financial confidence should be calm, not loud.

If something feels rushed or confusing, slow down. Real opportunities survive scrutiny.

Ten Common Financial Mistakes

1. Chasing quick wins instead of building systems
2. Ignoring fundamentals like budgeting and saving
3. Taking risks without understanding downside
4. Avoiding investing due to fear or confusion
5. Overreacting to market volatility
6. Carrying high-interest debt unnecessarily
7. Skipping protection like insurance
8. Delaying planning because life feels busy
9. Comparing progress to others
10. Acting emotionally instead of intentionally

These mistakes are common. None are fatal by themselves. Patterns are what cause damage.

Ten Rules for Long-Term Success

1. Stay disciplined when things feel boring
2. Build systems that work under pressure
3. Understand what you own and why
4. Respect risk without fearing it
5. Protect yourself before chasing growth

6. Let time and compounding work
7. Adjust intentionally, not emotionally
8. Ask for help when complexity increases
9. Ignore noise and focus on fundamentals
10. Stay in the game

These rules are simple, not easy. They work because they do not change.

The Investing Concept Explained Through the Sport

Advisors are coaches.

Scams are shortcuts.

Long-term success comes from fundamentals, discipline, and patience.

Athletes who chase shortcuts rarely last. Those who respect the process build careers.

Coach's Perspective: What Would Your Coach Say?

"Trust the process."

"Ask questions."

"Don't take shortcuts."

"Protect the locker room."

Financially, that means surrounding yourself with people who respect fundamentals, avoiding noise, and staying disciplined when excitement fades.

Game Situations and Decision Points

Situation one. A complex opportunity arises. Do you seek guidance or guess?

Situation two. Someone promises fast returns. Do you slow down or rush?

Situation three. Your plan feels boring but steady. Do you change it or trust it?

Each situation mirrors a late-season decision. Experience matters.

Common Athlete Mistakes and Financial Parallels

Athletes sometimes trust confidence over competence. Investors fall for hype.

Athletes sometimes avoid asking for help. Investors go it alone too long.

Athletes sometimes chase shortcuts. Investors chase returns.

Awareness corrects these patterns.

Winning the Long Game

Long-term success is not flashy.

It is built through discipline, humility, and consistency. It requires ignoring noise, respecting fundamentals, and making decisions aligned with values instead of emotion.

You do not need to be perfect. You need to stay engaged.

Winning the long game means protecting progress, staying coachable, and trusting that small, smart decisions repeated over time add up.

That is how athletes win careers. That is how money works too.

Athlete Takeaways

- Asking for help is a strength, not a weakness
- Scams rely on urgency and emotion
- Fundamentals beat shortcuts every time
- Discipline matters more than intelligence
- Stay in the game and trust the process

Chapter 26: Losing the Schedule and Rebuilding Structure

One of the hardest transitions for athletes has nothing to do with talent, effort, or intelligence.

It is losing the schedule.

For most of your life, someone else told you where to be and when. Workouts were mandatory. Practice times were set. Film sessions were scheduled. Meals, travel, lifts, meetings, and recovery all lived on a calendar you did not control.

That structure was invisible while you were in it. But once it disappears, the absence is loud.

Life gets harder when no one is setting your calendar. Not because you became lazy, but because structure was doing more work than you realized.

This chapter is about why the loss of structure quietly breaks financial habits and how to rebuild systems that replace mandatory discipline with intentional discipline.

From Mandatory Workouts to Optional Discipline

In sports, discipline is built into the environment.

You do not decide whether to train. Training is required. You do not debate whether to lift. It is scheduled. You do not negotiate rest days. They are planned. Accountability exists whether you feel motivated or not.

When sports end, discipline becomes optional.

No one forces you to wake up early. No one checks whether you trained. No one tracks your reps. The same shift happens financially.

Bills still exist. Saving still matters. Planning still matters. But without external structure, everything becomes optional. Optional discipline is much harder than mandatory discipline.

Athletes often blame themselves for struggling here.

They think they lost motivation. They think something is wrong with them. In reality, the environment changed. The system disappeared.

Discipline did not fail. The structure that supported it vanished.

Why Lack of Structure Quietly Breaks Financial Habits

Financial habits rely heavily on routine.

Saving happens when it is scheduled. Investing works when it is automatic. Reviewing finances works when it has a place on the calendar. Without structure, good intentions slowly erode.

The breakdown is subtle.

You mean to save later.

You plan to review accounts soon.

You will deal with that bill tomorrow.

You will get organized next month.

Nothing explodes immediately. That is why it is dangerous.

Just like missed reps do not show up overnight, financial drift takes time to notice. But eventually, stress increases. Accounts feel chaotic. Decisions feel reactive instead of intentional.

Athletes recognize this pattern.

When practice attendance becomes optional, performance slips. When recovery is unstructured, injuries increase. When film study disappears, mistakes repeat.

Money behaves the same way.

Without structure, even disciplined people struggle.

Why Motivation Is Not the Answer

Many people try to solve this problem with motivation.

They wait to feel ready. They promise to be more disciplined. They rely on willpower.

Athletes know this does not work.

You do not train only when motivated. You train because the system requires it. Motivation follows structure, not the other way around.

Financial discipline works the same way.

If saving depends on how you feel that month, it will fail. If investing depends on market mood, it will fail. If organization depends on free time magically appearing, it will fail.

Systems beat motivation every time.

Replacing Practice Schedules With Personal Systems

When sports end, structure must be rebuilt intentionally.

Not copied exactly, but replaced thoughtfully.

Think about what the old schedule did for you.

It removed decision-making.

It created consistency.

It enforced accountability.

It reduced mental load.

Your financial system should do the same.

Start with automation.

Automatic savings replaces mandatory workouts. Automatic investing replaces scheduled lifts. Bills on autopay replace coaches reminding you of responsibilities. Automation removes emotion and excuses.

Next, build review rituals.

Athletes reviewed film weekly. You need a money version of that. Monthly check-ins. Quarterly reviews. Annual planning sessions. These are not about judgment. They are about awareness.

Put them on the calendar. Non-negotiable.

Then, create constraints.

In sports, constraints exist everywhere. Time limits. Roster limits. Rules. Constraints create focus.

Financially, constraints look like spending plans, account separation, and clear priorities. When everything is flexible, discipline collapses. When boundaries exist, decisions get easier.

Finally, create accountability.

Athletes had coaches, teammates, and standards. After sports, accountability often disappears. Find ways to replace it.

A partner. A planner. A trusted friend. Even written commitments you revisit regularly. Accountability keeps structure alive when motivation fades.

Identity Loss and the Hidden Impact on Money

Losing the schedule is often tied to losing identity.

When you were an athlete, structure reinforced who you were. Once that disappears, money decisions start filling emotional gaps.

Overspending becomes reward.

Avoidance becomes protection.

Risk becomes excitement.

These behaviors are not about money. They are about structure and identity loss.

Rebuilding structure helps stabilize identity.

When days have rhythm again, money decisions feel calmer. When routines exist, impulsive behavior decreases. Structure creates emotional safety.

Athletes who rebuild structure recover faster in every area of life, not just finances.

The Investing Concept Explained Through the Sport

Structure is the invisible advantage.

Mandatory workouts created results long before game day. Scheduled practice built consistency. Systems made discipline repeatable.

Personal financial systems replace team schedules.

Automation replaces mandatory reps. Reviews replace film sessions. Boundaries replace rules. Accountability replaces coaches.

You do not need more effort. You need structure.

Coach's Perspective: What Would Your Coach Say?

A coach would be blunt.

"Discipline is a choice now."

"No one is coming to save you."

"Build your own system."

"Do the work anyway."

Financially, that means designing structure on purpose instead of hoping discipline magically appears. Coaches do not accept excuses when systems fail. Life will not either.

Game Situations and Decision Points

Situation one. Your schedule opens up after sports. Do you let days drift or create routines?

Situation two. Financial habits slip slowly. Do you blame motivation or rebuild structure?

Situation three. Life feels chaotic. Do you add complexity or simplify systems?

Each situation mirrors the same decision athletes face after sports. Do you drift, or do you design?

Common Athlete Mistakes and Financial Parallels

Athletes assume discipline should transfer automatically. Financial habits collapse without structure.

Athletes rely on motivation instead of systems. Saving and investing become inconsistent.

Athletes overestimate willpower. Burnout follows.

Awareness fixes these mistakes. Structure prevents them.

Winning the Long Game

The end of sports is not the end of discipline.

It is the beginning of self-directed discipline.

The athletes who thrive after sports are not the most talented. They are the ones who rebuild structure quickly. They replace external schedules with internal systems. They design routines that support long-term success.

Money responds the same way performance always did.

Consistency beats intensity.

Structure beats motivation.

Systems beat intention.

You do not need to recreate your old schedule.

You need a new one.

Build it. Protect it. Trust it.

That is how you win the long game after the whistle stops.

Athlete Takeaways

- Losing structure makes everything harder
- Optional discipline is harder than mandatory discipline
- Motivation fades, systems endure
- Automation replaces mandatory reps
- Rebuilding structure restores control and confidence

Chapter 27: From Teammates to Coworkers

One of the most disorienting transitions for athletes is not physical. It is cultural.

You go from a world where roles are clear, feedback is constant, and authority is obvious to one where expectations are vague, accountability is inconsistent, and success is often undefined. The uniform comes off. The locker room disappears. Suddenly, you are surrounded by coworkers instead of teammates.

The workplace can feel foreign after sports, not because athletes lack work ethic or discipline, but because the rules changed without being explained.

This chapter is about understanding that shift, adapting without losing yourself, and protecting income growth and career stability in an environment that plays by very different rules.

Why the Workplace Feels Foreign After Sports

In sports, clarity is built into the system.

You know who the coach is. You know who makes decisions. You know your role. You know when you are performing well and when you are not. Feedback is frequent. Accountability is visible. Effort is expected.

The workplace often lacks all of that.

Job descriptions are vague. Authority is layered and political. Performance reviews happen once or twice a year. Feedback is filtered, delayed, or absent.

Success is measured inconsistently. Expectations shift without notice.

For athletes, this feels unsettling.

You are used to earning trust through effort and execution. In many workplaces, effort is assumed, execution is subjective, and visibility matters more than results.

This does not mean the workplace is broken. It means it operates under a different logic.

Authority Without Coaches

Athletes are trained to respond to clear authority.

Coaches set standards. They correct mistakes. They decide playing time. Even when you disagree, you know where authority lives.

In the workplace, authority is often diffuse.

Your manager may not have final say. Decisions may come from people you never meet. Power may sit with personalities, tenure, or politics instead of performance. Accountability can feel uneven.

This creates confusion for athletes who are used to direct leadership.

You may wait for instruction that never comes. You may assume good work will automatically be recognized. You may expect correction that never happens.

Learning to navigate authority without coaches means becoming more proactive.

You must clarify expectations instead of waiting for them. You must seek feedback instead of assuming it will be given. You must manage up instead of relying on hierarchy.

This is not about changing who you are. It is about understanding the environment.

Feedback Without Film

Athletes live on feedback.

Film does not lie. Stats are visible. Performance is reviewed constantly. You know where you stand.

In the workplace, feedback is often sparse and indirect.

Silence may mean you are doing fine. Or it may mean no one is paying attention. Praise may be vague. Criticism may come late or indirectly. Performance reviews may focus on perception more than output.

This lack of feedback can be destabilizing.

Athletes may overwork to compensate. They may assume the worst. They may struggle to calibrate effort because signals are unclear.

The solution is intentional feedback loops.

Ask specific questions. Request clarity. Frame feedback as growth, not insecurity. Waiting passively for evaluation in a system that does not prioritize it puts income growth at risk.

Athletes who learn to replace film sessions with intentional conversations adapt faster.

Politics, Ambiguity, and Unclear Expectations

Sports are not free of politics, but performance usually wins in the end.

In many workplaces, politics never leave.

Decisions may be influenced by relationships, optics, timing, or agendas unrelated to performance. Expectations may change mid-project. Priorities may conflict. Accountability may be uneven.

This frustrates athletes who are wired for fairness and merit.

The mistake is assuming politics can be ignored.

Ignoring them does not make them disappear. It just makes you unaware.

Understanding workplace politics does not mean participating in them aggressively. It means recognizing dynamics, reading the room, and protecting your position.

Ambiguity is part of the system.

Clear instructions are rare. Success is often defined after the fact. Athletes who thrive learn to clarify goals early, document progress, and align their work with what leadership values, not just what feels productive.

How This Impacts Income Growth

Income growth in sports is often tied to performance and availability.

In the workplace, income growth is tied to visibility, leverage, timing, and negotiation as much as output.

Athletes who assume raises and promotions will arrive automatically often stall.

You may be working hard, producing results, and still be overlooked if decision-makers are unaware or misaligned. You may stay loyal to a role that no longer offers upside. You may undervalue your skills because feedback is unclear.

This is not failure. It is a system mismatch.

Athletes must learn to advocate for themselves without feeling disloyal or arrogant. They must understand how compensation decisions are made and who influences them. They must be willing to move when growth stalls.

Income growth is not selfish. It is stability.

Career Stability in a Non-Team Environment

Teams in sports are bonded by shared goals.

Workplaces often are not.

Coworkers may compete for recognition. Incentives may conflict. Loyalty may be conditional. Layoffs, restructures, and reorganizations happen without warning.

Athletes often assume team dynamics translate directly. They expect mutual support and shared sacrifice. When that does not happen, disappointment follows.

Career stability comes from adaptability, not loyalty alone.

Building transferable skills. Maintaining professional relationships.

Keeping financial flexibility. Understanding your value in the market.

Athletes are good at this once they recognize the shift.

You trained your body to adapt. You can train your career the same way.

The Investing Concept Explained Through the Sport

Moving from teammates to coworkers is a league change.

The rules are different. The field is different. The referees are inconsistent. Talent still matters, but awareness and adaptability matter more.

Income growth depends on understanding the system, not fighting it.

Career stability depends on positioning, not comfort.

Coach's Perspective: What Would Your Coach Say?

A coach would be direct.

"Figure out the rules."

"Do not assume."

"Communicate."

"Protect yourself."

Financially, that means understanding how your workplace actually works and adjusting behavior accordingly. Coaches prepare players for different opponents. You must prepare for different environments.

Game Situations and Decision Points

Situation one. You are working hard but receiving little feedback. Do you wait or ask for clarity?

Situation two. You feel underpaid but uncomfortable advocating. Do you stay silent or prepare a case?

Situation three. The workplace culture feels unstable. Do you hope it improves or build optionality?

Each situation mirrors an athlete adjusting to a new league.

Common Athlete Mistakes and Financial Parallels

Athletes assume effort equals reward. Income growth stalls.

Athletes wait for instruction. Opportunities pass.

Athletes avoid politics entirely. Visibility suffers.

These are not character flaws. They are transition gaps.

Winning the Long Game

The move from teammates to coworkers is one of the biggest adjustments athletes face.

It requires new skills without abandoning old strengths.

Work ethic still matters. Discipline still matters. Coachability still matters. But awareness, communication, and self-advocacy now matter just as much.

Those who adapt protect income growth, reduce financial stress, and build long-term stability.

Learn the rules of the new league.

Stay composed.

Be intentional.

That is how you build a career that lasts after the locker room fades.

Athlete Takeaways

- The workplace plays by different rules than sports
- Authority and feedback are often unclear
- Politics exist whether you engage or not
- Income growth requires visibility and advocacy
- Adaptability creates career stability

Chapter 28: When No One Is Watching Anymore

One of the most uncomfortable moments for former athletes comes quietly.

There is no buzzer. No final whistle. No announcement. One day, you realize no one is watching anymore.

No coaches checking attendance.

No teammates holding you accountable.

No scoreboard reflecting effort.

No crowd reacting to your performance.

For years, pressure created structure. Accountability created discipline. Someone was always watching, evaluating, correcting, and pushing. When that disappears, a gap opens. Not because athletes stop caring, but because the environment that enforced standards is gone.

This chapter is about that discipline gap, why it leads to self-sabotage for so many former athletes, and how money mistakes often show up years later as a result.

The Discipline Gap After Accountability Disappears

In sports, discipline is rarely optional.

You lift because it is scheduled. You condition because it is required. You show up because someone notices when you do not. Accountability is built into the system.

When sports end, accountability becomes invisible.

No one tracks your habits. No one knows if you skipped a workout, overspent, avoided a hard conversation, or procrastinated on planning. The absence of pressure feels like freedom at first.

But freedom without structure often turns into drift.

Athletes are conditioned to perform under observation. Remove the observation without replacing the structure, and discipline weakens. This is not a character flaw. It is an environmental shift.

Money is one of the first places this shows up.

Bills get paid eventually. Saving gets delayed. Investing becomes inconsistent. Decisions that once would have been corrected quickly now linger. Nothing explodes right away, which makes the drift harder to notice.

The discipline gap is quiet. That is what makes it dangerous.

Why Former Athletes Self-Sabotage Without Pressure

Self-sabotage sounds dramatic, but it often looks ordinary.

Spending a little too much because you deserve it.

Avoiding financial organization because it feels tedious.

Taking unnecessary risks because boredom creeps in.

Ignoring problems because they are not urgent yet.

Without pressure, some athletes unconsciously create chaos.

They chase intensity because intensity used to equal meaning. When life feels flat, risky decisions can feel alive. Big purchases. Big bets. Big changes. Not because they make sense, but because they recreate adrenaline.

Others move in the opposite direction.

They avoid discomfort entirely. They choose ease over growth. They delay decisions that require effort or uncertainty. They tell themselves they will handle it later.

Both paths lead to the same place.

Lost momentum.

Athletes were trained to respond to pressure, not to design their own. When no one is watching, some struggle to hold themselves to standards they never had to self-enforce before.

Comfort vs Growth Decisions

In sports, comfort is rarely rewarded.

Growth lives in discomfort. Extra reps. Tough feedback. Conditioning when tired. You accepted this because growth was visible and reinforced.

After sports, comfort becomes seductive.

Sleeping in. Spending for convenience. Avoiding planning. Choosing familiarity over challenge. None of these decisions feel wrong in isolation. Over time, they compound.

Financially, comfort decisions often look like this.

Choosing lifestyle upgrades instead of saving.

Keeping money scattered because organization feels annoying.

Avoiding long-term planning because it feels abstract.

Staying in stagnant roles because change feels risky.

Growth decisions feel different.

They are quieter. They require patience. They lack immediate reward. They feel invisible because no one applauds discipline in private.

Former athletes often struggle here because growth used to be public.

Now it is private.

Choosing growth when no one is watching is the real test.

Translating "Grind Culture" Into Adult Life

Grind culture worked in sports because it was contained.

There was an off-season. There were recovery periods. There were coaches who monitored load. There was a clear objective.

In adult life, grind culture without structure becomes burnout.

Working nonstop. Chasing income without boundaries. Filling time to avoid stillness. Confusing busyness with progress. Athletes know how to work hard. They are often terrible at pacing themselves without external limits.

Money suffers when grind culture is misapplied.

People earn more but save less. Stress increases even as income rises. Decisions become reactive. There is movement, but no direction.

The lesson is not to abandon discipline.

It is to redefine it.

Adult discipline is not about grinding endlessly. It is about consistency, systems, and recovery. It is about doing the boring things well for a long time.

Training your finances requires a different type of toughness.

Quiet toughness.

Why Money Mistakes Show Up Years Later

Money mistakes rarely punish immediately.

That is why they are easy to make.

Skipping savings does not hurt today.

Ignoring investing feels harmless early.

Carrying small debt balances seems manageable.

Avoiding planning feels neutral.

Years pass. Then the cost shows up.

Stress increases. Options shrink. Opportunities feel limited. The gap between where you are and where you expected to be feels confusing and unfair.

Former athletes often say, "I do not know how this happened."

It happened slowly.

Just like conditioning loss does not show up in one missed workout, financial consequences emerge after long periods of drift.

The absence of immediate feedback is the problem.

In sports, mistakes are corrected quickly. In money, mistakes compound quietly.

The Investing Concept Explained Through the Sport

This phase is like training without a coach.

No one sets reps. No one tracks progress. No one calls you out. The athletes who succeed are the ones who internalize standards and build systems that replace external accountability.

Discipline becomes self-directed.

Structure becomes intentional.

Money reflects this shift faster than almost anything else.

Coach's Perspective: What Would Your Coach Say?

A coach would not sugarcoat this.

"No one is coming to save you."

"Standards do not disappear just because supervision does."

"Do the work anyway."

"Discipline is who you are when no one is watching."

Financially, that means holding yourself accountable even when outcomes are delayed. Coaches know championships are won in empty gyms. Wealth is built the same way.

Game Situations and Decision Points

Situation one. You get a raise. Do you increase lifestyle or strengthen foundations?

Situation two. No one checks your finances. Do you avoid organization or build systems?

Situation three. Life feels flat. Do you chase risk for excitement or commit to growth?

Each situation asks the same question.

Who are you when no one is watching?

Common Athlete Mistakes and Financial Parallels

Athletes confuse pressure with purpose. Money decisions become reckless.

Athletes choose comfort after years of grind. Financial discipline erodes.

Athletes assume effort will always be rewarded. Planning gets delayed.

These mistakes are understandable. They are also correctable.

Winning the Long Game

The end of sports removes the audience.

It does not remove the opportunity.

The athletes who thrive long term are the ones who redefine discipline. They replace external pressure with internal standards. They stop chasing intensity and start building consistency.

Money rewards that shift.

Quiet habits. Clear systems. Intentional choices. Discipline without applause.

You do not need someone watching.

You need standards you respect.

That is how growth continues long after the crowd is gone.

Athlete Takeaways

- Discipline weakens when accountability disappears
- Self-sabotage often replaces pressure
- Comfort choices compound quietly
- Grind culture must evolve to avoid burnout
- Money mistakes appear years after habits form

Chapter 29: Redefining Winning After the Uniform Comes Off

When you are an athlete, winning is obvious.

The scoreboard tells you. The record confirms it. Film backs it up. Success and failure are visible, measurable, and immediate. You know where you stand because the game tells you.

When the uniform comes off, that clarity disappears.

There is no official scoreboard for adulthood. No rankings released weekly. No coach pulling you aside to say where you stand. That absence creates a vacuum, and many former athletes fill it the only way they know how.

They keep chasing something to beat.

This chapter is about why status often replaces performance after sports, how that shift shows up in money and career decisions, and how to build a new definition of winning that actually fits life in your 30s and 40s.

Why Chasing Status Replaces Chasing Performance

In sports, performance is rewarded directly.

If you train well, execute well, and compete well, outcomes usually follow. The feedback loop is tight. Effort connects to results in a way that is easy to see.

After sports, performance becomes harder to measure.

You can work hard and still feel invisible. You can perform well and receive little feedback. Progress is slower. Recognition is inconsistent.

That uncertainty is uncomfortable for people who grew up in merit-based systems.

Status fills that gap.

Titles. Income. Job prestige. Square footage. Cars. Neighborhoods. These become proxies for performance because they are visible. They create a sense of winning when internal measures feel unclear.

This is not vanity. It is adaptation.

Former athletes are wired to compete. When the original competition ends, the instinct does not disappear. It just looks for a new arena.

The problem is that status is a poor replacement for performance.

Status compares you to others. Performance compares you to your own standards. One builds anxiety. The other builds confidence.

Income vs Fulfillment

Income matters.

It provides security, options, and stability. Pretending money does not matter is unrealistic. But income alone is not fulfillment.

Many former athletes chase income the same way they once chased wins. More is better. Faster is better. Bigger numbers feel like progress.

Then something strange happens.

Income increases, but satisfaction does not. Stress rises. Time shrinks. Relationships strain. The scoreboard says you are winning, but it does not feel that way.

That disconnect creates confusion.

Athletes are used to sacrifice paying off clearly. In adult life, sacrifice without alignment leads to burnout.

Fulfillment comes from alignment.

Work that uses your strengths. Schedules that support health. Income that reduces pressure instead of creating it. Progress toward goals that matter to you, not just ones that look good from the outside.

Income supports fulfillment. It does not replace it.

Titles, Houses, Cars, and Comparison Traps

Status symbols are seductive because they are easy to measure.

Job titles feel like rankings. Houses feel like trophies. Cars feel like proof. Social media amplifies all of it.

Former athletes are especially vulnerable here because comparison used to be productive.

You compared stats. You compared records. You compared performance to improve. After sports, comparison often turns toxic because context disappears.

You do not see debt.

You do not see stress.

You do not see tradeoffs.

You only see outcomes.

That creates pressure to keep up instead of choosing intentionally. Decisions become reactive. Lifestyle expands faster than clarity. Financial commitments pile up in service of appearances.

Athletes understand how dangerous this is on the field.

Playing someone else's game never works. Chasing another player's role creates mistakes. Financially, chasing someone else's version of success does the same.

Comparison is a terrible coach.

What Success Actually Looks Like in Your 30s and 40s

Success evolves.

In your 20s, success may look like opportunity and momentum. In your 30s and 40s, it often looks different.

Control over your time.

Consistency in your health.

Confidence in your finances.

Presence in your relationships.

Progress toward goals that matter.

This kind of success is quieter.

There are fewer trophies. Less applause. More responsibility. But it is also more sustainable.

Former athletes sometimes struggle here because the feedback loop is slower.

You do not get immediate validation for making disciplined choices. You feel the benefits years later. That requires trust in the process, something athletes actually understand deeply, even if it feels different.

You trained for seasons, not days.

You trusted coaches before results showed.

You built foundations before championships appeared.

Adult success works the same way.

Building a New Scoreboard

If you do not build your own scoreboard, you will borrow someone else's.

That borrowed scoreboard will almost always prioritize status over substance.

Building a new scoreboard means deciding what winning actually means now.

Ask different questions.

Do I have margin in my life, or am I constantly stretched?

Does my money reduce stress or amplify it?

Do my daily habits support the person I want to be in ten years?

Am I growing, or just staying busy?

Do I feel in control of my choices?

These are harder to quantify, but they are far more meaningful.

Athletes thrive when expectations are clear.

Your new scoreboard should be just as clear, even if no one else sees it.

The Investing Concept Explained Through the Sport

Redefining winning is a league change.

The rules are different. The metrics are different. The crowd is quieter. But competition still exists.

Now you compete against drift, distraction, and default decisions.

Winning is not about beating others. It is about executing your plan consistently over time.

Coach's Perspective: What Would Your Coach Say?

A coach would reframe the mission.

"Define success clearly."

"Stop playing someone else's game."

"Win the reps that matter."

"Trust the process."

Financially, that means aligning money decisions with your values, not your ego. Coaches hate when players chase stats instead of wins. The same applies here.

Game Situations and Decision Points

Situation one. You are offered a higher-paying role that costs health and time. Do you chase income or protect balance?

Situation two. You feel behind compared to peers. Do you expand lifestyle or refocus on foundations?

Situation three. Your life looks successful but feels empty. Do you double down or reassess?

Each situation asks the same question.

What does winning mean now?

Common Athlete Mistakes and Financial Parallels

Athletes replace performance with status. Money decisions become image-driven.

Athletes chase validation externally. Fulfillment erodes.

Athletes assume winning should feel the same forever. Frustration grows.

These are not failures. They are transition points.

Winning the Long Game

Winning after sports is not louder.

It is clearer.

It is defined by freedom, alignment, and control. By progress you respect, not applause you chase. By building a life that supports who you are becoming, not who you used to be.

You already know how to do this.

You trained for years without guarantees. You trusted systems. You played for something bigger than one moment.

Do the same now.

Redefine the scoreboard.

Play the long game.

Win on your terms.

Athlete Takeaways

- Status often replaces performance after sports
- Income supports fulfillment, it does not define it
- Comparison traps create pressure, not clarity
- Success evolves in your 30s and 40s
- Build a new scoreboard that fits your life

Chapter 30: Staying Connected Without Living in the Past

When sports end, one of the biggest losses is not routine or identity.

It is connection.

Teams create instant community. Shared goals. Shared struggle. Shared language. You see the same people every day. You suffer together. You compete together. You win and lose together. That kind of connection is rare in adult life, and when it disappears, the absence can be jarring.

Former athletes often underestimate this loss.

They expect to miss competition. They expect to miss routine. They rarely expect how quiet life can feel without the locker room.

This chapter is about staying connected without getting stuck. About honoring where you came from while continuing to move forward.

Why Isolation Hits Former Athletes Hard

Athletes are conditioned to belong.

From a young age, teams become social centers. Friends overlap with teammates. Coaches overlap with mentors. Identity overlaps with role. Even introverted athletes are surrounded by people who understand them without explanation.

When that environment ends, isolation can hit suddenly.

Workplaces rarely provide the same depth of connection. Social circles fragment. Schedules diverge. People stop showing up automatically. If you do not actively create connection, it slowly disappears.

This isolation often shows up indirectly.

Drifting motivation. Increased spending for stimulation. Overworking. Numbing behaviors. Constant nostalgia. None of these are random. They are attempts to replace lost connection.

Athletes are not weak for feeling this. They are human.

Community was built into the system before. Now it must be built intentionally.

The Role of Community, Mentorship, and New Locker Rooms

Connection does not have to disappear. It has to evolve.

Former athletes often look for replacement teams that feel exactly the same. That rarely works. Adult communities are different. They are less intense, less centralized, and less automatic. But they can still be meaningful.

New locker rooms look different.

Professional communities. Volunteer organizations. Faith groups. Fitness communities. Alumni networks. Mentorship circles. These spaces may not recreate the old environment, but they can provide shared values and mutual accountability.

Mentorship becomes especially important.

In sports, mentors were assigned. Coaches existed by default. After sports, mentorship must be sought. That can feel uncomfortable at first, but it is a skill worth developing.

Strong mentors provide perspective. They shorten learning curves. They remind you that transition is normal, not failure.

Athletes understand coaching better than most. Applying that mindset to adult life creates connection and growth.

Finding Purpose Without the Team

Teams provide built-in purpose.

You know why you train. You know what the goal is. You know how your role contributes to something bigger. When sports end, that clarity often disappears.

Purpose does not vanish. It just becomes less obvious.

Many former athletes chase purpose by replicating intensity. They overcommit to work. They chase money. They seek adrenaline. These paths can work temporarily, but they often lead to burnout because they are substitutes, not solutions.

Purpose after sports is quieter.

It may come from mentorship. Building something. Serving others. Mastering a craft. Being present for family. Contributing consistently rather than dramatically.

Athletes sometimes struggle here because purpose used to be public.

Now it is private.

That does not make it smaller. It makes it more personal.

Purpose does not need a scoreboard to matter.

Healthy Nostalgia vs Being Stuck

Nostalgia is natural.

Missing teammates. Remembering big moments. Telling old stories. None of this is a problem. Sports were meaningful. Pretending they were not does not help anyone.

The issue is not nostalgia.

The issue is when nostalgia becomes the primary identity.

Healthy nostalgia honors the past while leaving room for growth. Being stuck uses the past as a hiding place.

You can usually tell the difference.

Healthy nostalgia coexists with curiosity about the future. Being stuck resists change. Healthy nostalgia fuels gratitude. Being stuck fuels comparison and regret.

Athletes sometimes replay the highlight reel because the future feels uncertain.

That makes sense.

But growth requires forward motion.

You are not abandoning your past by building something new. You are honoring it by using what it taught you.

Creating a Forward-Looking Identity

Identity in sports was often assigned.

You were the captain. The defender. The scorer. The grinder. Roles were clear and reinforced daily. After sports, identity becomes self-directed.

That freedom can feel overwhelming.

Without intentional identity building, people default to old labels or external validation. Former athlete becomes the entire story. Or job title replaces it. Neither fully works.

A forward-looking identity is built, not inherited.

It asks different questions.

Who am I becoming?

What values guide my decisions now?

What strengths do I want to keep using?

What new skills do I want to develop?

Athletes already know how to do this.

You reinvented yourself at different levels. Youth to high school. High school to college. College to beyond. Each transition required adaptation. This one is no different.

The difference is that no one is assigning the role anymore.

You get to choose it.

The Investing Concept Explained Through the Sport

Connection is infrastructure.

Teams provide it automatically. After sports, you must build it intentionally. Without it, motivation fades and decision-making suffers. With it, discipline and purpose return.

Staying connected without living in the past is like transitioning leagues.

The rules change. The pace changes. But the fundamentals still apply.

Community matters.

Mentorship accelerates growth.

Identity evolves.

Coach's Perspective: What Would Your Coach Say?

A coach would be honest.

"Do not isolate."

"Stay connected."

"Keep growing."

"Do not peak early."

Financially and emotionally, isolation creates blind spots. Coaches hate when players disappear after setbacks. Life works the same way.

Stay in the game, even if the game looks different now.

Game Situations and Decision Points

Situation one. You miss the locker room and feel disconnected. Do you withdraw or seek new community?

Situation two. You constantly relive the past. Do you honor it and move forward or stay stuck?

Situation three. You feel unsure who you are without sports. Do you avoid the question or start building intentionally?

Each situation asks the same thing.

Will you design connection, or wait for it to return?

Common Athlete Mistakes and Financial Parallels

Athletes isolate when structure disappears. Motivation drops.

Athletes cling to past identity. Growth stalls.

Athletes avoid new environments because they feel unfamiliar. Opportunity shrinks.

These patterns are understandable. They are also changeable.

Winning the Long Game

Staying connected does not mean living in the past.

It means carrying forward what mattered most.

Discipline. Loyalty. Teamwork. Resilience. These qualities did not expire when the uniform came off.

They are tools for the next chapter.

Build new locker rooms. Seek mentors. Lead where you can. Stay curious about who you are becoming.

You are not done competing.

You are just competing in a different arena now.

Athlete Takeaways

- Isolation is common after sports and must be addressed intentionally
- New locker rooms look different but still matter
- Purpose becomes quieter but more personal
- Nostalgia is healthy when it does not block growth
- Build a forward-looking identity, not a backward-facing one

Glossary of Softball and Financial Terms

This glossary connects key financial concepts to familiar ideas from **softball**, making money easier to understand through the language, structure, and discipline athletes already know. The goal is not memorization. It is recognition. If you understand the game, you already understand more about money than you think.

Asset Allocation

Financial Definition:

How money is divided among different investment types such as stocks, bonds, and cash to balance risk and return.

Softball Comparison:

How responsibility, difficulty, and timing are distributed within a lineup or game plan. Too much focus on one area without balance creates instability.

Assets

Financial Definition:

Things you own that have value, such as cash, investments, real estate, or retirement accounts.

Softball Comparison:

Your strengths as a player. Skills, conditioning, experience, and preparation that contribute to overall performance.

Bonds

Financial Definition:

Loans made to governments or companies that pay interest and return principal over time.

Softball Comparison:

Defense and fundamentals. Not flashy, but essential for stability when pressure increases.

Budget

Financial Definition:

A plan for how income is allocated toward expenses, savings, and goals.

Softball Comparison:

Pitch counts or play calls. Without knowing the timing, execution breaks down.

Cash Flow

Financial Definition:

Money coming in versus money going out.

Softball Comparison:

Energy management. If you burn too much early, you struggle to finish strong.

Compounding

Financial Definition:

Earnings that generate additional earnings over time.

Softball Comparison:

Reps and muscle memory. Each rep builds on the last and makes progress easier over time.

Credit

Financial Definition:

The ability to borrow money with the promise of repayment.

Softball Comparison:

Trust with a coach. When earned and managed well, it gives you opportunities. When abused, it costs you playing time.

Debt

Financial Definition:

Money borrowed that must be repaid, often with interest.

Softball Comparison:

Extra weight in your equipment bag. Manageable in small amounts, dangerous when excessive.

Diversification

Financial Definition:

Spreading investments across different assets to reduce risk.

Softball Comparison:

Not relying on one hitter or one pitcher to carry the entire game.

Emergency Fund

Financial Definition:

Savings set aside for unexpected expenses.

Softball Comparison:

Backup gloves or extra cleats. You hope you never need them, but they save the day when something breaks.

ETF (Exchange-Traded Fund)

Financial Definition:

A fund that holds many investments and trades like a stock.

Softball Comparison:

A deep roster instead of a solo player.

Fees / Expense Ratios

Financial Definition:

Costs associated with managing investments.

Softball Comparison:

Mental errors or sloppy transitions. Small issues that quietly drain momentum over time.

Growth Investing

Financial Definition:

Investing in companies expected to grow faster than average.

Softball Comparison:

High-upside recruits. More potential, more volatility, and a need for patience.

Insurance

Financial Definition:

Protection against financial loss from unexpected events.

Softball Comparison:

Protective gear. You do not play without it when risk increases.

Liquidity

Financial Definition:

How easily money can be accessed without penalty or delay.

Softball Comparison:

In-game flexibility. The ability to adjust quickly when conditions change.

Net Worth

Financial Definition:

Assets minus liabilities.

Softball Comparison:

The final score after the season, not one at-bat.

Rebalancing

Financial Definition:

Adjusting investments back to their intended mix over time.

Softball Comparison:

Between-inning adjustments to restore balance and execution.

Risk

Financial Definition:

The chance that outcomes differ from expectations, including loss.

Softball Comparison:

Difficulty selection. Higher reward often comes with higher risk.

Roth IRA

Financial Definition:

A retirement account where money grows tax-free if rules are followed.

Softball Comparison:

Front-loaded conditioning so the late innings feel easier.

Stocks

Financial Definition:
Ownership shares in a company.
Softball Comparison:
Primary playmakers. They drive offense but need support to win.

Tax-Advantaged Accounts

Financial Definition:
Accounts that provide tax benefits, often with rules and restrictions.
Softball Comparison:
Structured training programs. Rules exist to improve outcomes, not restrict progress.

Volatility

Financial Definition:
Short-term ups and downs in market value.
Softball Comparison:
A wobble on a hard-hit ball. Normal movement unless you panic.

Permanent Loss

Financial Definition:
Money that cannot recover due to poor decisions or panic.
Softball Comparison:
A fall after abandoning fundamentals.

Total Return

Financial Definition:

Investment return from both price growth and income.

Softball Comparison:

The full box score. Every contribution matters.

Value Investing

Financial Definition:

Investing in assets believed to be undervalued.

Softball Comparison:

Clean execution. Less flash, more control, consistent results.

Yield

Financial Definition:

Income generated from an investment.

Softball Comparison:

Consistent run production. Not dramatic, but reliable.

Final Note

This glossary reinforces one core principle:

Financial success, like success in softball, comes from balance, discipline, timing, and repetition.

That philosophy runs through **Softball Money 101** and extends far beyond the field and competition.

Disclaimers

Educational Purpose Only

This book is for educational purposes only.

The information provided in **Softball Money 101** is intended to help readers understand general financial concepts using softball-based analogies. It is not individualized financial, investment, tax, legal, or insurance advice.

Every financial situation is different. Your goals, income, family circumstances, risk tolerance, and time horizon are unique. What works for one athlete or family may not be appropriate for another.

Not Financial, Investment, Tax, or Legal Advice

Nothing in this book should be interpreted as a recommendation to buy, sell, or hold any specific investment, financial product, account type, or strategy.

This book does not replace advice from qualified professionals, including but not limited to:

- Financial advisors
- Accountants or tax professionals
- Attorneys
- Insurance professionals

Before making financial decisions, readers should consult professionals who can evaluate their individual situation and provide personalized guidance.

No Guarantees or Promises of Results

All investing involves risk, including the possible loss of principal.

Past performance does not guarantee future results. Markets fluctuate. Economic conditions change. Outcomes cannot be predicted or guaranteed.

The examples, scenarios, and illustrations in this book are hypothetical and for educational purposes only. They may not reflect actual results or real-world outcomes.

Tax and Legal Information

Any discussion of taxes, retirement accounts, estate planning, or legal structures is general in nature.

Tax laws and regulations change frequently and vary by jurisdiction. Legal requirements differ based on location and personal circumstances.

Readers should seek personalized tax or legal advice before acting on any information related to these topics.

Athlete and Career Considerations

This book discusses financial topics as they relate to athletes and former athletes, including career transitions, income changes, and life after sports.

It does not provide career placement services, employment advice, or guarantees related to income, compensation, or career success.

Use of Analogies

Softball and sports analogies are used throughout this book to make financial concepts easier to understand.

These analogies are educational tools only and should not be interpreted literally. Financial decisions require analysis beyond analogy and comparison.

Personal Responsibility

By reading this book, you acknowledge that:

- You are responsible for your own financial decisions
- You understand that financial outcomes involve uncertainty
- You agree to seek appropriate professional guidance when needed

Education can improve decision-making, but responsibility remains with the individual.

Contact Information

If you would like to learn more about the concepts discussed in this book or explore additional educational resources, Pat Brown can be found through public platforms including LinkedIn, Twitter, and via Google search.

For questions specifically related to **Softball Money 101**, you may contact Pat Brown at:

info@softballmoney101.com

Final Reminder

Financial success is built over time through discipline, planning, and consistency.

This book provides a framework, not a guarantee.

Use it as a guide, not as a substitute for professional advice.

Pat Brown OLB, University of Kansas

Made in the USA
Monee, IL
04 November 2026

67376101R00118